Equality and Gender Roles

ISSUES

Volume 221

Series Editor

Lisa Firth

 *Independence*

Educational Publishers

Cambridge

First published by Independence

The Studio, High Green

Great Shelford

Cambridge CB22 5EG

England

© Independence 2012

British Library Cataloguing in Publication Data

A sustainable future. -- (Issues ; 218)

1. Nature--Effect of human beings on. 2. Environmental

responsibility. 3. Sustainability.

I. Series II. Firth, Lisa.

363.7-dc23

ISBN-13: 978 1 86168 606 0

LC35651
305.3
ESOGC

Printed in Great Britain

MWL Print Group Ltd

CONTENTS

OTHER TITLES IN THE ISSUES SERIES

For more on these titles, visit: www.independence.co.uk

A note on critical evaluation

Because the information reprinted here is from a number of different sources, readers should bear in mind the origin of the text and whether the source is likely to have a particular bias when presenting information (just as they would if undertaking their own research). It is hoped that, as you read about the many aspects of the issues explored in this book, you will critically evaluate the information presented. It is important that you decide whether you are being presented with facts or opinions. Does the writer give a biased or an unbiased report? If an opinion is being expressed, do you agree with the writer?

Equality and Gender Roles offers a useful starting point for those who need convenient access to information about the many issues involved. However, it is only a starting point. Following each article is a URL to the relevant organisation's website, which you may wish to visit for further information.

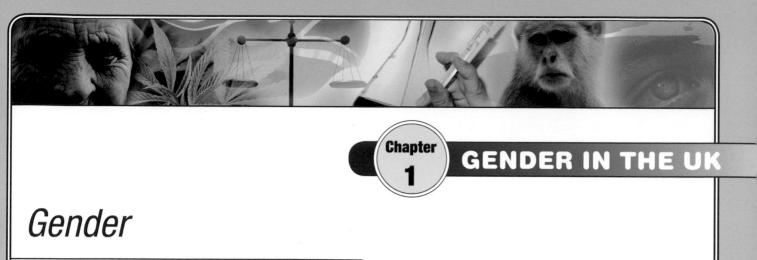

Gender

If somebody told you, 'You really don't count,' what would you think? Is it right to dismiss half the human race?

What is it?

Sexual identity, especially in relation to society or culture; the condition of being female or male.

Gender refers to socially-constructed roles and learned behaviours and expectations associated with females and males. When talking about gender, people usually talk about gender inequality – women and girls having fewer opportunities in life simply because they are female. The term gender, however, also refers to boys and men, who are equally defined by the rights and roles 'assigned' to them. Giving equal rights and consideration to girls and women should not take the same away from males.

> **In societies that care equally for the wellbeing of men, women and children, it's easier for poor people to climb out of poverty and improve their standard of living**

While women worldwide have made great strides to prove they are as smart and capable as men, in many countries they are still not treated as equals. Girls and women aren't given the same rights, opportunities, responsibilities and choices in life that boys and men consider their birthright.

Why should I care?

Women represent half of the world's population. This double standard for girls and women hurts everyone in society and has a negative impact on economic development. Societies in which women have equal rights are wealthier. These countries prosper more, grow faster and have better governance systems, which are important for growth and development.

Conversely, inequalities between women and men tend to be largest among the poor, according to *Engendering Development*, a World Bank publication that talks about the importance of gender for development.

In some Indian villages, men are likely to spend a big portion of their income for personal use (such as smoking, drinking, gambling) while the women devote all of their income to family needs (such as food, medical treatment, school fees and children's clothing), according to an Indian study cited in *Voices of the Poor*, a collection of interviews of more than 60,000 poor women and men around the world.

In Africa, where most people earn a living by working in agriculture, women do at least 70% of farm work. Yet they have very little say in how this income gets spent. And when women aren't allowed to make decisions on how to use financial income to help their families, it becomes more difficult to help poor people climb out of poverty, explains Mark Blackden, gender specialist at the World Bank. The situation becomes even more critical in households headed by women. The lack of access to legal, economic and social services often leaves them poorer.

If countries in South Asia, Africa and the Middle East had equally schooled boys and girls like East Asian countries did between 1960 and 1992, their income per capita would likely have grown an additional 0.5−0.9% per year, according to World Bank research.

In societies that care equally for the wellbeing of men, women and children, it's easier for poor people to climb out of poverty and improve their standard of living.

Lifecycle of inequality

Around the globe, there are females who will spend a lifetime being denied:

⇨ Personal freedom – In some countries, like Ghana, women are legally their husband's property, while in others, women cannot leave the house or get a job without a man's permission, according to *Voices of the Poor*.

⇨ Education – Fewer girls than boys enrol in or complete primary or secondary schooling, even though research shows investing in girls' education significantly improves a country's economic outlook.

⇨ Jobs or equal pay – Labour laws and regulations in several developing countries actively discourage women from working. When they get a job, women can expect to earn up to 27% less than men for the same job – regardless of experience and education.

⇨ Legal rights – Limited legal standing impacts females in countless ways – from the inability to borrow money because they can't legally own land, to the inability to make decisions regarding how their children are cared for, to the inability to decide when and how to be touched. When women are legally and therefore economically dependent upon their spouses or other male relatives, they have very little choice but to accept what is granted them in life. For example, in Ukraine, Latvia and Macedonia, where there are laws against rape, women say they don't bother to report rape because of lack of action by authorities.

⇨ Political representation – Women are under-represented at all levels of government everywhere in developing countries, despite being capable of representing their people. Without representation, there is very little attention drawn to laws that limit opportunities for girls and women.

Breaking barriers proves difficult

Fighting gender discrimination can be difficult because it can go against entrenched local traditions. So, while laws may be revised, people continue to live by deeply-held cultural beliefs.

For example, in the 1960s India outlawed the tradition of dowry – where a husband demands that his bride comes with material possessions or he won't take her as a wife. But this tradition is so entrenched in local society that most brides still provide dowry. Things are slowly changing. You might have heard in the news of cases where brides are rebelling against this practice and reporting it to the authorities.

What is the international community doing?

At the Fourth World Conference on Women in Beijing in 1995, the international community agreed on a Platform for Action to improve the lives of women and girls. The conference participants realised that development and progress aren't possible if half of a country's population is not considered equal.

The World Bank and other organisations working on development have become strong advocates for gender equality in all aspects of life. The Bank has provided about $6.3 billion since 1995 for girls' education and more than two-thirds of its loans for health, nutrition and population have included gender-related objectives. Additional projects address legal reforms designed to strengthen women's access to legal rights, especially the right to own land.

The World Bank's Gender Action Plan (GAP), started in 2007, has been working towards advancing women's economic empowerment throughout the world. As of January 2009, the GAP has allocated $29.3 million toward accomplishing its goal.

The international community has also started to look at issues that boys face. For example, in some Central European, Latin American and Caribbean countries, many boys are dropping out of school, especially secondary school. They often don't see the benefit of staying in school, and instead prefer to find work, but are often lured by jobs related to various illegal activities.

What can I do?

If you are a girl or a woman, never stop believing that your voice is valuable and your contribution is needed to improve the world around you. Stay in school and pursue your dreams no matter how hard the road to success may be. If you are a boy or a man, respect women as you respect yourself. Be conscientious of subtle inequalities.

⇨ The above information is reprinted with kind permission from uthink! Visit http://youthink.worldbank.org for more information.

© World Bank

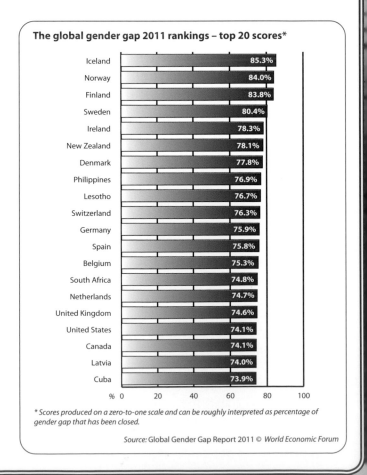

The global gender gap 2011 rankings – top 20 scores*

Iceland	85.3%
Norway	84.0%
Finland	83.8%
Sweden	80.4%
Ireland	78.3%
New Zealand	78.1%
Denmark	77.8%
Philippines	76.9%
Lesotho	76.7%
Switzerland	76.3%
Germany	75.9%
Spain	75.8%
Belgium	75.3%
South Africa	74.8%
Netherlands	74.7%
United Kingdom	74.6%
United States	74.1%
Canada	74.1%
Latvia	74.0%
Cuba	73.9%

*Scores produced on a zero-to-one scale and can be roughly interpreted as percentage of gender gap that has been closed.

Source: Global Gender Gap Report 2011 © World Economic Forum

WORLD BANK

Questions about the Equality Act 2010

What is the purpose of the new Act?

The Equality Act 2010 brings together a number of existing laws into one place so that it is easier to use. It sets out the personal characteristics that are protected by the law and the behaviour that is unlawful. Simplifying legislation and harmonising protection for all of the characteristics covered will help Britain become a fairer society, improve public services, and help business perform well. A copy of the Equality Act 2010 and the explanatory notes that accompany it can be found on the Home Office website (www.homeoffice.gov.uk).

Who is protected by the Act?

Everyone in Britain is protected by the Act. The 'protected characteristics' under the Act are (in alphabetical order):

⇨ Age;

⇨ Disability;

⇨ Gender reassignment;

⇨ Marriage and civil partnership;

⇨ Pregnancy and maternity;

⇨ Race;

⇨ Religion and belief;

⇨ Sex;

⇨ Sexual orientation.

What behaviour is unlawful?

Under the Act people are not allowed to discriminate against, harass or victimise another person because they have any of the protected characteristics. There is also protection against discrimination where someone is perceived to have one of the protected characteristics or where they are associated with someone who has a protected characteristic.

⇨ Discrimination means treating one person worse than another because of a protected characteristic (known as direct discrimination) or putting in place a rule or policy or way of doing things that has a worse impact on someone with a protected characteristic than someone without one, when this cannot be objectively justified (known as indirect discrimination).

⇨ Harassment includes unwanted conduct related to a protected characteristic which has the purpose or effect of violating someone's dignity or which creates a hostile, degrading, humiliating or offensive environment for someone with a protected characteristic.

⇨ Victimisation is treating someone unfavourably because they have taken (or might be taking) action under the Equality Act or supporting somebody who is doing so.

Who has a responsibility under the Act?

⇨ Government departments;

⇨ Service providers;

⇨ Employers;

⇨ Education providers (Schools, FHE colleges and Universities);

⇨ Providers of public functions;

⇨ Associations and membership bodies;

⇨ Transport providers.

What's new?

Most of the new Equality Act was already in place in the previous anti-discrimination laws that it replaces. This includes the Race Relations Act 1976, the Sex Discrimination Act 1975, and the Disability Discrimination Act 1995. In total there are nine pieces of primary legislation and over 100 pieces of secondary legislation being incorporated. Bringing it into one piece of legislation will make the law easier to understand and apply.

As the Act is an amalgamation and harmonisation of existing law, there aren't many massive changes. For example, indirect discrimination is being extended to apply to disability and gender reassignment for the first time. The prohibition on direct discrimination on grounds of pregnancy and maternity and gender reassignment will apply in schools for the first time. The Act also introduces some new provisions, such as the prohibition on discrimination arising from disability.

When does the new Equality Act come into force?

The Government Equalities Office says 90 per cent of the law came into force on 1 October 2010. The remaining ten per cent has been set to one side by the Government because it wants to consider in more detail how it might work. It is up to the Government to decide when these parts of the Act will be implemented. More information about the implementation of the Equality Act can be found on the Home Office website.

⇨ The above information is reprinted with kind permission from the Equality and Human Rights Commission: www.equalityhumanrights.com

EQUALITY AND HUMAN RIGHTS COMMISSION

'Family man'

British fathers' journey to the centre of the kitchen.

By Adrienne Burgess, Head of Research, Fatherhood Institute

> 'Because my wife works, I don't need to put in the long hours my father did. My children are teenagers now and we've been close right from the beginning. We have these massive rows with time to make up and talk things through. I don't know why anyone would do it – work such long hours they don't have time for all that. I feel sorry for most men: they don't know what it's like to be at the centre of the kitchen.'
>
> Terry, 49, father-of-two

The OCADO research

In light of the clear associations between uptake of paternity leave and involved fatherhood; and between involved fatherhood and men's greater participation in family work, including childcare, cooking and shopping – plus the new entitlement of 'additional paternity leave' available to fathers whose babies are due on or after 3 April 2011 – OCADO decided to commission research.

This, among other things, asked questions never asked before about UK fathers' uptake of paternity leave, as well as their attitudes and plans relating to additional paternity leave. So what are the headline findings?

Paternity leave

Our survey identified 60% of fathers now taking, or having taken, paternity leave – with another 23% planning to take it in the future. This accords with other studies. Of the men who hadn't taken paternity leave we were not surprised to find that 29% had been unable to afford to take it or had not been eligible.

What we were startled to discover was that 15% had not known about their entitlement to simple paternity leave although it has been available to them since 2003 – and another 8% had been told by their employer that they were not to take it. This last, of course, is illegal.

The other surprise – and this was a positive one – was that only 6% of the men who hadn't taken paternity leave had felt that taking it would have damaged their career prospects. This was a worry for men a decade ago – but times are clearly changing.

Additional paternity leave

Here the men's knowledge-base was even lower – perhaps not surprisingly, since the entitlement is a new one: 54% did not know they could take over the second six months of their partner's maternity leave. Most, however, were glad to hear it, with 81% supporting this new opportunity for couples to share the care of their baby in the first year. And about the same percentage as worried that taking paternity leave would damage their career prospects felt the same about additional paternity leave: a third of the 16% of men who would not take additional paternity leave saw their employer's or their manager's negative attitude as a barrier.

Clearly, government policy is moving in the right direction – and perhaps even faster than the politicians think: in 2005, when the idea of additional paternity leave was mooted, the Government estimated that between 92% and 96% of new fathers would not take it up. The fathers in our survey had different ideas: only 16% said they would not take any of the leave, with 21% keen to take the whole six months, and another 47% interested in taking between one and five months. 28% of the fathers who would not take additional paternity leave said they could not afford for either themselves or their partner to take more than six months' leave in total, with another 26% saying they earn more than their partner or have better career prospects (9%) so taking the leave didn't make financial sense.

Where the men would take additional paternity leave (the vast majority), 55% would take the leave because they want to look after their baby themselves, with 43% also seeing this as benefiting their child. Perhaps most importantly from an employer's point of view, 51% of the men said that their taking over the leave would enable their partner to go back to work earlier than she otherwise would have done – and only 21% said this would not be the case. Further, while 22% of the men felt that their partner's employment prospects would be damaged by taking six months' maternity leave, 30% felt that her employment prospects would suffer if she took the full 12 months.

Indeed, women's long-term absence from the workplace on maternity leave does profoundly damage their careers and is also difficult for employers. Thus it seems that fathers' uptake of additional paternity leave, though it will take some men out of the workforce for a short time, will more often than not benefit their partner and her employer, who will have her back at work earlier. And when women can continue to play a greater part at work, and are employed at their skill and education levels, the economy – as well as the women themselves, and their family – benefits. Interestingly, while 50% of the men felt that taking six months' leave to look after

their baby would damage their career prospects, only 22% felt that taking similar leave would damage their partner's. They may well be wrong.

Men feel they are capable – but society doesn't see it that way

Among men who would not take additional paternity leave, only 8% gave as a reason that they would not feel confident taking care of their baby alone, with only 4% worried that they might feel isolated at home. Two out of three of all our interviewees believe they would be as competent caregivers as their partner; and 45% say that if they were to announce to family and friends that they were taking six months' additional paternity leave they would actually feel proud, with only 13% saying they would feel embarrassed. Most feel trusted by their baby's mother, too, with only 2% saying that would not be the case.

However, as far as 'outsiders' are concerned, perceptions are different: almost two out of three men agreed or strongly agreed with the statement that 'the general public don't trust men to care for babies as much as they trust women to do this'. And almost half were clear that, in becoming fathers, they had been pretty well ignored by maternity services, with only one father in four feeling that had not been the case. Only 43% of the men felt that ante-natal classes had been really good at helping them prepare to be a father.

It's often thought that mothers are more profoundly emotionally affected by parenthood than fathers are – for example, missing their children more when they are apart for a sustained period. However, only 30% of our fathers thought this would be true in their case, with 17% saying they believe they actually miss their children more than their partner does, and 53% saying that both parents miss them 'about the same'.

Fathers would be willing to go that extra mile

Research shows that when men believe an activity relating to their children is very good for their development, they will do their best to take part. Our survey showed great willingness by the great majority of fathers to do so. Asked whether 'if you knew for sure that it would help your child succeed in life' they would go to parenting classes or relationship counselling and so on, most of the fathers said 'yes': 50% would be willing to go to parenting classes, 40% to take part in relationship counselling, 54% to spend more time in their child's school, and 65% to read more with their child at home. Since fathers' taking part in any or all these activities actually does benefit their children substantially, this suggests that if teachers and others approach fathers in the right way, they will find willing participants. When asked whether they would use a voucher for a free parenting course, 60% of the fathers said 'yes'; while only 27% would be willing to work longer hours – even if they knew that would benefit their child.

In conclusion

It seems that the Government's policy of moving towards more equal distribution of parenting leave is in tune with the times: fathers are very interested in taking leave – and they want this leave so they can be closer to their children and because they believe it's good for them. They feel competent at caring for their children, are trusted by their partner to do so and feel sufficiently connected into their communities not to feel they would get isolated or distressed spending time as 'principal carer'. A massive percentage would get more involved with their children's schools and spend more time reading with their children at home if they were convinced this really mattered. A sizeable proportion would even go for parenting classes and relationship counselling.

BUT a lot of the men are unaware of the leave entitlements available to them – even simple paternity leave. They feel they are not trusted or valued as carers by the wider community and that this starts right at the beginning – during their partner's pregnancy when ante-natal services discount them or fail to provide them with the information and support that they need to be good dads and support their partners well.

Some of their employers are behind the times, too. They won't let male employees take leave to which they are entitled and are more likely to make them pay a career-penalty if they do take leave than would be the case if they were a woman.

What is plain is that, against the odds, today's dads are contributing substantially at home to their children's care – and will do more as this is made possible for them. Retailers, teachers, family services and others should take note: there are huge opportunities for schools and nurseries to get fathers more involved if they approach them in the right way, with respect for what they have to offer and with recognition of the extent to which they are passionate about their children's wellbeing. And businesses that have done very well marketing their services and products to mothers are going to have to broaden their offer to include both parents if they are to succeed in this new parenting landscape.

Most fathers are not yet at the centre of the kitchen – but they're heading that way.

12 June 2011

⇨ The above information is an extract from the Fatherhood Institute's research summary *'Family Man': British Fathers' Journey To the Centre of the Kitchen*, and is reprinted with permission. Visit www.fatherhoodinstitute.org for more information on this and other related topics.

© Fatherhood Institute

THE FATHERHOOD INSTITUTE

Why women are still left doing most of the housework

An Oxford University study says if current trends continue, women will probably have to wait until 2050 before men are doing an equal share of the household chores and childcare. According to the paper published in the latest issue of the journal Sociology, 'substantial and persistent obstacles' remain.

The international study, conducted by the ESRC-funded Centre for Time Use Research at Oxford, has analysed more than 348,000 diary days from 20- to 59-year-olds in 16 countries. It finds that we are in the middle of a 70- to 80-year trend towards equality in housework and caring.

Barriers to equality include the gender-specific view of whether certain household chores were 'men's' or 'women's work'. 'Routine housework' such as cleaning, cooking and caring for family members is viewed as 'feminine' while 'masculine' roles include non-routine chores like DIY, car care and outside work.

The amount of time women spend on routine housework still dwarfs time spent on non-routine domestic jobs carried out by men. Nevertheless, there is evidence to show that the gender gap in housework and childcare has been narrowing gradually. Women's time spent on caring and chores in the home declined gradually from about 360 minutes a day in the 1960s for both the UK and US to 280 and 272 minutes, respectively, in the early 2000s. In the UK and the US, men went from spending 90 and 105 minutes a day, respectively, on housework and childcare in the 1960s to 148 and 173 minutes in the early part of this millennium. However, the data suggests that the upward trend for men may have levelled off in some countries in recent years.

Dr Oriel Sullivan, a Research Reader from the Department of Sociology, said: 'Even though women are still responsible for the major share of unpaid work, studies suggest that the gender gap in the time spent doing both paid and unpaid work is closing slowly. We've looked at what is hampering equality in the home, and we have found that certain tasks seem to be allocated according to whether they are viewed as "men's" or "women's work". Employment and childcare policies also play a part: in those countries where women are regarded as full members of the primary labour force – as in the Nordic countries – rather than mums or home-makers, there is greater gender equality in the sharing of domestic work too.'

'Child care is an interesting contrast to routine housework because for both men and women, the time that's spent in childcare has been increasing quite dramatically, contrary to many media panics about the effect that women moving into employment in large numbers would have on child development and the time children get to spend with their parents,' added Dr Sullivan.

Nordic countries where employment policies encourage women to enter the labour force by providing better maternity and paternity leave and public childcare services were found to have greater equality in the sharing of domestic tasks at home. The UK, like the US, Canada and Australia, is governed more by market forces than by egalitarian social policy and, according to the study, this does not provide the same level of equality for women in the workplace or at home. The growth of the service sector, which relies heavily on shift work and long or fragmented hours, tends to reinforce traditional gender roles in the home, as housework has to be done on a routine basis and does not match well with the men's long working weeks, the study suggests.

> *'Routine housework' such as cleaning, cooking and caring for family members is viewed as 'feminine' while 'masculine' roles include non-routine chores like DIY, car care and outside work*

Co-author Professor Jonathan Gershuny, Director of the Centre for Time Use Research at the University of Oxford, said: 'Despite equality in educational access and in legal requirements for equality in the workplace, women still take a primary role in domestic work. Men are doing more, but their contribution is primarily in the defined "masculine" non-routine tasks in the home.'

23 May 2011

⇨ The above information is reprinted with kind permission from the University of Oxford. Visit www.ox.ac.uk for more information.

© University of Oxford

Are pink toys turning girls into passive princesses?

The colour-coding of toys – pink for girls and blue for boys – reinforces pernicious gender stereotypes, says Kat Arney.

Last month US clothing retailer J Crew released photos showing the company's president, Jenna Lyons, painting her five-year-old child's toenails their favourite shade of hot pink. No big deal, you might think, until you notice the child is a boy.

The ensuing media kerfuffle highlights what anyone from a toddler to Dame Barbara Cartland could have told you. Pink is a girl's colour, and is certainly not fit for a boy's toenails.

Take a trip to a toy store and you'll see this gender divide writ large in the aisles. On one side, the boys' toys – Lego and other construction kits, pirate costumes, toy guns, racing cars and so on – boxed in blue and other 'manly' colours and illustrated with pictures of boys.

Turn a corner, and you're assaulted by a wall of pink built from Barbie dolls, multi-packs of miniature high heels, princess outfits and tea sets.

The message is clear: these are boys' toys, and those are girls' toys. And in this particular battle of the sexes, there's very little neutral territory.

Many people – such as the Pink Stinks campaign – are fighting against the power of pink. In response to complaints about the pink/blue divide in their wares, toy retailer the Early Learning Centre points vaguely to research showing that 'gender is a major factor in determining children's colour preferences, with most boys typically preferring blue and girls preferring pink from infancy'.

But is this really true? And does it even matter? Together with radio producer Jolyon Jenkins, I've been searching for the scientific truth behind the rampant pinkification of toys for girls.

Perhaps the most compelling evidence that 'pink is for girls' comes from colour preference studies where children or adults are asked to look at different colours and pick their favourite. The earliest example of this kind of experiment was conducted at the Chicago World's Fair in 1893 and suggested that most people prefer blue, with a slight female preference for redder hues.

Fast-forward to 2007, when Professor Anya Hurlbert's experiments appeared to show the same thing: adult women prefer redder colours than do men.

Hurlbert suggests that women may be more attuned to red thanks to our evolutionary ancestry as berry gatherers, enabling us to spot ripe fruit among the greenery. This 'scientific proof that girls prefer pink' was widely reported in the media and was derided by those who prefer their *Just So Stories* penned by Rudyard Kipling rather than serious academics.

The fact remains that most tests of colour preference do show at least a slight female leaning towards redder colours. However, virtually all of these studies have been carried out in adults or children over the age of three – an age by which a child is already aware of its own gender, and is exquisitely sensitive to cues from its parents and peers (as anyone who has watched in horror as their toddler mimics them knows only too well).

The biggest study of colour preference in younger children tells a different story. Professor Melissa Hines

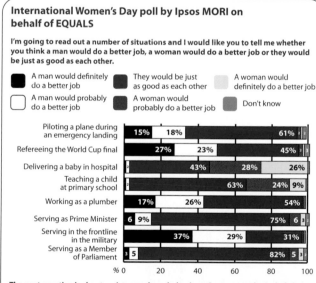

International Women's Day poll by Ipsos MORI on behalf of EQUALS

I'm going to read out a number of situations and I would like you to tell me whether you think a man would do a better job, a woman would do a better job or they would be just as good as each other.

- A man would definitely do a better job
- A man would probably do a better job
- They would be just as good as each other
- A woman would probably do a better job
- A woman would definitely do a better job
- Don't know

Piloting a plane during an emergency landing	15%	18%	61% 2 3
Refereeing the World Cup final	27%	23%	45% 3
Delivering a baby in hospital	43%	28%	26%
Teaching a child at primary school	63%	24%	9%
Working as a plumber	17%	26%	54%
Serving as Prime Minister	6 9%	75%	6 3
Serving in the frontline in the military	37%	29%	31%
Serving as a Member of Parliament	3 5	82%	5 3

% 0   20   40   60   80   100

The next question is about sexist remarks or behaviour. Some examples include being whistled at, having sexist comments directed at you, being touched inappropriately or being discriminated against because of your gender, but you may have experienced something different. In the last five years, have you PERSONALLY experienced sexist remarks or behaviour DIRECTED AT YOU in any of the following places?

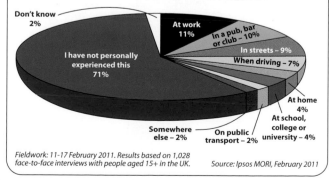

- Don't know 2%
- At work 11%
- In a pub, bar or club – 10%
- In streets – 9%
- When driving – 7%
- I have not personally experienced this 71%
- At home 4%
- At school, college or university – 4%
- On public transport – 2%
- Somewhere else – 2%

Fieldwork: 11-17 February 2011. Results based on 1,028 face-to-face interviews with people aged 15+ in the UK.   *Source: Ipsos MORI, February 2011*

THE GUARDIAN

ran tests on more than 100 children under the age of two and found no difference in colour preference, with both sexes preferring pinker colours – possibly because that's the colour of Mummy.

But a difference did show up in the types of toys kids preferred. Boys as young as 12 months old tended to go for moving toys like cars and balls, while girls picked dolls. Intriguingly, this finding also bears up in non-humans. Male rhesus monkeys prefer to play with balls and toy cars, while females are drawn to dolls.

It seems likely that even if there isn't an innate girlie preference for pink, there is a gender bias in the types of toys boys and girls prefer. But it's important to remember that this isn't an exclusive divide. Girls still like playing with cars and construction toys, while boys enjoy playing with dolls. After all, what is Action Man if not a dolly with a crew cut?

So why the proliferation of pink in the toy aisles? Colour researcher Stephen Palmer thinks he might have the answer. He has been investigating how people respond to colour on an emotional level, associating different things – both negative and positive – with different colours.

His study suggests that adults lean towards clean, blue colours (reminiscent of clean water or sunny skies) and shun yellowy-brown or khaki shades that remind us of unpleasant things, such as faeces or vomit.

He also found that it's relatively easy to twist people's colour preferences, depending on how they feel about objects of a particular colour. Giving people differently coloured sweet- or bitter-tasting drinks can skew their colour preferences. And you can shift someone towards or away from liking red by showing them either pictures of tasty berries and cherries, or yucky blood and guts.

The same link between personal preferences and colour also shows up outside the lab. Students at the University of California, Berkeley – whose branding is blue and gold – show stronger preferences for those shades than the colours of UCB's arch-rival Stanford University (team colours red and white), and vice versa.

If this holds true for children's toys, then it could simply be that girls like pink because the things they like (regardless of their colour) are pink, and there's no underlying biological reason for the rampant pinkification of their toys.

Does it actually matter? Considering everything I've found out about this subject recently, I can't help feeling that it does.

The increasing separation of toys into 'for boys' and 'for girls', strongly coded by colour and reinforced by highly gendered marketing, is depriving girls of active toys and games that encourage the development of their spatial and analytical skills.

Instead, they're pushed towards being passive princesses, surrounded by fashion dolls, kiddie make-up and miniaturised vacuum cleaners. And at the same time, boys are denied opportunities for more social and imaginative play.

In a society that is fighting hard for equal rights for both sexes, it seems a retrograde step to be increasingly forcing our kids into these pink and blue stereotypes. Isn't it about time we stemmed the tide of pink?

Kat Arney is a broadcaster and science information officer for Cancer Research UK.
9 May 2011

© Guardian News and Media Limited 2011

Girls don't want to be princesses. They want to be hot

Disney has pulled the plug on princesses. After its current release, Tangled, there are no more plans for fairy tales of this long-popular ilk. The reason? A studio worker has reportedly said that from the age of five 'girls no longer want to be princesses. They want to be hot.'

By Una Purdie, WVoN co-editor

Five-year-old girls already striving to be 'sexually exciting or excited' is a worrying development, but not a surprising one.

Sexualised imagery has become a normal backdrop to children's lives. The bombardment comes from every angle, and takes many forms; from the less-than-subtle, direct marketing of sex-industry related goods, such as pole-dancing toys and Playboy-branded pencil cases, to the narrow, sexualised role of women and girls in films, music videos and magazines.

The age of models is also getting younger; witness the images in last December's *Vogue Paris*. Heavily made-up girls as young as six years old, sprawled on beds in high-heels, surrounded by leopard skin.

Sexualised imagery has become a normal backdrop to children's lives

Is this innocent dressing-up, or sending the message that they are mini-adults and sexually available?

In what an Australian Research Institute paper called 'corporate paedophilia', girls are being given a clear message from an early age: their bodies are sexual commodities, and their value depends on how well they use them.

Having another talent is not enough. When even the most stalwart of female role models for girls – British children's TV *Blue Peter* presenters – are expected to pose topless for lads' mags, we know we're in deep.

Pornography has slipped from the top shelves quietly into mainstream entertainment, and the objectified view of women is the image that sticks in girls' minds.

42-year-old mother-of-four and social worker Amy Henderson discussed experiences in her family:

'Overtly sexualised images have always been around, but it's just absolutely everywhere now. It really affects how girls see themselves, and boys too. The Internet doesn't help – they see hardcore stuff we just weren't exposed to, and frequently.'

Henderson's eyes were opened to the extent of the problem when she found her 12-year-old daughter was sending texts, or 'sexting', naked images of herself in explicit sexual poses to her boyfriend of the same age.

The abusive style of language with which he used to address her was straight from a porn handbook. It went way beyond what she considered normal teenage sexual experimentation:

'I found a lot of young girls were feeling pressure to perform sexual acts seen in porn films – more violent-edged, degrading stuff. They think they have to do these things before they even know anything about relationships. It's disturbing.'

This not only impacts on the self-worth of the girls, it can have tragic consequences. Another pupil at the same school as Henderson's daughter had sexually provocative photographs of her taken by a group of boys.

They consequently plastered them all over the Internet, branding her a 'slut' and a 'whore'. She committed suicide.

Linda Thomson of the Glasgow-based Women's Support Project hears many similar stories: 'It's not just that the technology is available for "sexting", it's the expectation that's the issue.'

Thomson works primarily in the area of commercial sexual exploitation and has found challenging underlying societal attitudes a key part of her work.

A recent survey of 1,000 young girls aged 15 to 19 found 63% considered 'glamour model' to be their ideal profession. A quarter thought lap dancing was a good choice, while only 4% chose teaching

---

'I work with groups of young women aged 12 to 16 and they see no other value for women apart from whether somebody wants to have sex with them or not.

'They have internalised the messages and don't see any alternative. One girl told me last week how amazing it must be to be a lap dancer, all those men wanting to have sex with you.'

A recent survey of 1,000 young girls aged 15 to 19 found 63% considered 'glamour model' to be their ideal profession. A quarter thought lap dancing was a good choice, while only 4% chose teaching.

Thomson believes a lack of counterbalance in what children see worsens the problem. There is very little health education programming on television, and even fewer alternative aspirational role models in the mainstream media. As a result, gender stereotypes deepen.

'It's the commercialisation of sex, the business of sex, that is dictating to us how we should be. All rites of passage have been sexualised. No stag night is complete now without a lap dancer.

'Look at the adverts in lads' mags – their expected leisure time entertainment is all about the sex industry now.

'It's hard also for young men. How do they grasp the notion of anything but enthusiastic consent? To be a young man is to be a porn consumer, and if you're uncomfortable with it, then you can't open your mouth because you're accused of being effeminate, not quite a man or somehow weird. That doesn't say much about choice.'

Speaking up is an issue for parents too. While Thomson gives a cautious welcome to the higher political and media profile recently given to the issues, she is concerned about how the topic is framed.

The concerns are often simplistically linked with a right-wing, censorial agenda rather than the liberal left. Speaking out can lead to accusations of being 'prudish', when it's quite the opposite:

'No-one is saying young people should not be interested in sex – of course they should be. We're coming at it from the angle of equality and respect. Look at the gender stereotypes – are these progressive?

'No, it's narrow and restrictive – you can be sexy as long as you fit in their narrow agenda. Where the only power for a woman is to get naked for a camera – it's a transitory, fleeting power.'

9 March 2011

⇨ The above information is reprinted with kind permission from The Vibe. Visit www.the-vibe.co.uk for more information.

© The Vibe

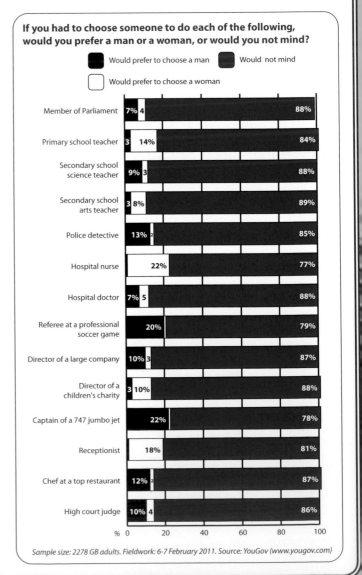

If you had to choose someone to do each of the following, would you prefer a man or a woman, or would you not mind?

■ Would prefer to choose a man   ■ Would not mind
□ Would prefer to choose a woman

	Prefer man	Not mind	Prefer woman
Member of Parliament	7%	88%	4
Primary school teacher	3	84%	14%
Secondary school science teacher	9%	88%	3
Secondary school arts teacher	3	89%	8%
Police detective	13%	85%	2
Hospital nurse		77%	22%
Hospital doctor	7%	88%	5
Referee at a professional soccer game	20%	79%	
Director of a large company	10%	87%	3
Director of a children's charity	3	88%	10%
Captain of a 747 jumbo jet	22%	78%	
Receptionist		81%	18%
Chef at a top restaurant	12%	87%	2
High court judge	10%	86%	4

% 0   20   40   60   80   100

Sample size: 2278 GB adults. Fieldwork: 6-7 February 2011. Source: YouGov (www.yougov.com)

THE VIBE

Stop sexual bullying

What are 'gender equality' and 'sexual bullying'?

What is gender?

It is important to understand that 'gender' is more than just biology: it is something we learn from those around us, who present us with their understanding of what it means to be a girl or a boy. Most of us see the following as stereotypes but, at the same time, find ourselves accepting them and rarely challenge them:

⇨ 'Boys are just more aggressive than girls.'

⇨ 'Girls like to shop and boys like to play football.'

⇨ 'Boys are better at science and girls are better at English.'

⇨ 'Boys don't cry and girls are bitchy.'

⇨ 'Women are better at looking after children than men.'

Women's average pay is 21% less than men's

Many young men feel they have to be good at sport and should not show or talk about their feelings. While many young women feel they are judged mainly by how they look, and feel they should be very girly or feminine to be attractive. People assume girls and boys think and act like this because of their biological differences. However, these biological differences do not mean that these stereotypes are true! It is the way the media and others around us talk about what it is to be male or female that makes us think these differences in abilities and characteristics are true.

What is gender inequality?

Although many of us are told we can achieve anything and be anything we want, being male or female will affect many of the choices we are offered and the decisions we take about our lives. Today, men and women are still not equal.

⇨ Women's average pay is 21% less than men's.

⇨ White British, working-class young men are least likely to do well at school.

⇨ Girls and young women are more likely to be physically, emotionally or sexually hurt.

What is sexual bullying?

It includes a range of behaviours such as sexualised name-calling and verbal abuse, rubbishing sexual performance, ridiculing physical appearance, criticising sexual behaviour, spreading rumours about someone's sexuality or sexual experiences they have had or not had, unwanted touching and physical assault. Sexual bullying is behaviour which is repeated over time and intends to victimise someone by using that person's gender, sexuality or sexual (in)experience to hurt them.

Research suggests girls and young women are more likely to experience sexual bullying, but many young men also report being judged and ridiculed for being 'gay', a 'sissy', not 'hard' enough or not sexually active.

> 'You have to show how masculine you are; you can't show sensitivity – it is difficult to be different – you need to look and act a certain way.'
>
> Young man, Year 11

Many young men feel they have to be good at sport and should not show or talk about their feelings. While many young women feel they are judged mainly by how they look

Ground rules

Remember – when talking about bullying, violence, discrimination or other experiences which people might find upsetting or which might make them feel uncomfortable – you should lay down some ground rules!

⇨ Treat people the way that you would want to be treated – with respect.

⇨ Don't promise to keep something someone tells you confidential – if you are concerned that someone in your school may be being hurt or is at risk of being hurt, you need to tell a member of staff.

⇨ Listen – give others the space and time to tell you what they think and about their experiences.

⇨ The above information is an extract from the Womankind report *Preventing violence, Promoting equality* and is reprinted with permission. Visit www.womankind.org.uk for more information.

© Womankind 2010

WOMANKIND

'SlutWalks' spark debate

Three in five Brits think 'SlutWalking' is not a good way to advance women's rights.

By Alice Moran

Three in five Brits say that the 'SlutWalk' protests, the name given to recent rallies in which women have claimed the right to wear what they want without being harassed by men, are not a good way to advance the cause of women's rights, our survey has revealed.

And although more than half of British people believe that women who dress in a sexually provocative way are not responsible if they're sexually harassed, over a quarter of people say that women who dress in a more suggestive way are responsible, with three-quarters saying that they are also more likely to be harassed.

⇨ 57% of Brits believe that women are not responsible if they dress in a sexually provocative way.

⇨ But 27% of Brits believe that women who dress in this way are responsible if they are sexually harassed.

Over a quarter of people say that women who dress in a more suggestive way are responsible [if they're sexually harassed]

⇨ Nearly three-quarters of people (73%) say that women who dress in a sexually provocative way are more likely to be harassed, while 14% disagree.

⇨ A sizeable 61% of people do not think that the recent spate of 'slut walking' is a good way to advance women's rights.

⇨ While just one in five people (20%) think that the protests help the cause of women's rights.

The recent spate of 'SlutWalks' began in Canada following one Toronto policeman's ill-judged comment that women could avoid rape if they didn't dress like 'sluts'. Thousands of people across Canada, the USA and Britain have marched in protest, with many dressing in purposefully provocative attire. The protesters hope to put focus upon the current mindset, which they say blames the victim, rather than the abuser, for sexual crimes.

On Saturday, up to 5,000 people took part in London's 'slut walk', as women in stockings, bras and basques proudly exhibited placards scrawled with statements such as 'Cleavage is not consent', 'It's a dress, not a "Yes"', and 'Hijabs, hoodies, hotpants; our bodies, our choices'. While the original march was sparked by events in Canada, Justice Secretary Ken Clarke unwittingly fuelled the angry sentiment behind the marches when he was forced to apologise after appearing to suggest some rapes were not as serious as others during a BBC interview last month.

15 June 2011

⇨ The above information is reprinted with kind permission from YouGov. Visit www.yougov.com for more information.

© YouGov

Women's representation

The proportion of women in politics, public appointments and on the boards of companies.

Women's representation

⇨ 51 per cent of the population are women.

⇨ 5.6 per cent of the population are Black, Asian and minority ethnic women (source: *ONS Experimental 2007 Population Estimates by Ethnic Group*. It is estimated that the percentage of females that define themselves outside the categories of 'White British', 'White Irish' and White Other' is 5.56 per cent of the total population of England and Wales).

⇨ Ten per cent of the population are disabled women.

Women in politics

⇨ 22.2 per cent of Members of Parliament are women (source: Parliament website as at March 2011).

⇨ 1.2 per cent of MPs are Black, Asian and minority ethnic women (data on the ethnicity of Members of Parliament is not routinely collected. This figure is based on information in the public domain).

⇨ 0.3 per cent of MPs are out lesbian (data on the sexual orientation of Members of Parliament is not routinely collected. This figure is based on information in the public domain).

⇨ 30.8 per cent of local councillors in England are women (source: *National Census of Local Authority Councillors 2008*).

⇨ 0.8 per cent of local councillors in England are Black, Asian and minority ethnic women (source: *National Census of Local Authority Councillors 2008*).

⇨ 46.7 per cent of Welsh Assembly members are women (source: Welsh Assembly Government as at March 2011).

⇨ 34.8 per cent of Scottish Parliament members are women (source: Scottish Government as at March 2011).

⇨ 13.8 per cent of Northern Ireland Assembly members are women (source: Northern Ireland website as at March 2011).

⇨ 31.9 per cent of UK members of the European Parliament are women (source: UK Office of the European Parliament website as at March 2011).

UK position in Europe and internationally

⇨ The UK is now placed 50th out of 188 countries worldwide in the national league table of women's representation in Parliament and 12th out of 27 countries in the European Union (source: Inter-Parliamentary Union website. The IPU is the international organisation of parliaments established in 1889. It provides comparative data on the percentage of women in each national parliament).

Women in public appointments

⇨ 32.6 per cent of public appointments are held by women (source: *Cabinet Office Public Bodies 2009*).

⇨ 50 per cent aspirational target for new public

THE HOME OFFICE

appointments to be held by women by 2015 (source: *The Equality Strategy – Building a Fairer Britain 2010*. The Government has set a new aspiration that by 2015, 50 per cent of new public appointments to public boards will be women).

⇨ 6.9 per cent of public appointments were held by members of minority ethnic groups. Of these, around 38 per cent were women.

⇨ 3.5 per cent of public appointments were held by disabled people. Of these, around 37 per cent were women.

Women on boards

⇨ 12.5 per cent of directors in FTSE 100 companies are women (source: *Female FTSE Report 2010*).

⇨ 13 per cent of newly appointed FTSE 100 directors are women (source: *Female FTSE Report 2010*).

⇨ 21 per cent of FTSE 100 companies with exclusively male boards (source: *Female FTSE Report 2010*).

⇨ 7.8 per cent of directors in FTSE 250 companies are women (source: *Female FTSE Report 2010*).

⇨ 5.5 per cent of FTSE 100 directors are from ethnic minority backgrounds (source: *Female FTSE Report 2010*).

⇨ 5.5 per cent of FTSE 100 Executive Directors are women (source: *Female FTSE Report 2010*).

⇨ 15.6 per cent of FTSE 100 non-executive directors are female (source: *Female FTSE Report 2010*).

Women in the public sector

⇨ 50 per cent of permanent secretaries in the civil service are women (source: *The Guardian* 4 March 2011)

⇨ 26.7 per cent of women in top 200 for civil service (source: Cabinet Office as at 31 March 2010).

⇨ 21.3 per cent of local authority chief executives are women (source: *JNCs for Chief Executives and Chief Officers annual surveys 2009* for CEs in England and Wales. Data includes directors and chief officers who report directly to the chief executive).

⇨ 14.3 per cent of senior police officers are women (source: Home Office statistics, police service strength as at 31 March 2010 for Chief Inspector and above).

⇨ The above information is reprinted with kind permission from the Home Office. Visit http://homeoffice.gov.uk for more information.

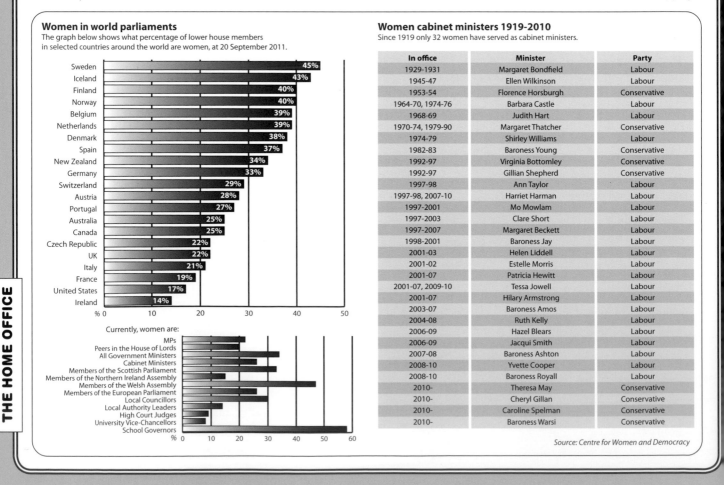

Women in world parliaments
The graph below shows what percentage of lower house members in selected countries around the world are women, at 20 September 2011.

Sweden 45%
Iceland 43%
Finland 40%
Norway 40%
Belgium 39%
Netherlands 39%
Denmark 38%
Spain 37%
New Zealand 34%
Germany 33%
Switzerland 29%
Austria 28%
Portugal 27%
Australia 25%
Canada 25%
Czech Republic 22%
UK 22%
Italy 21%
France 19%
United States 17%
Ireland 14%

Currently, women are:
MPs
Peers in the House of Lords
All Government Ministers
Cabinet Ministers
Members of the Scottish Parliament
Members of the Northern Ireland Assembly
Members of the Welsh Assembly
Members of the European Parliament
Local Councillors
Local Authority Leaders
High Court Judges
University Vice-Chancellors
School Governors

Women cabinet ministers 1919-2010
Since 1919 only 32 women have served as cabinet ministers.

In office	Minister	Party
1929-1931	Margaret Bondfield	Labour
1945-47	Ellen Wilkinson	Labour
1953-54	Florence Horsburgh	Conservative
1964-70, 1974-76	Barbara Castle	Labour
1968-69	Judith Hart	Labour
1970-74, 1979-90	Margaret Thatcher	Conservative
1974-79	Shirley Williams	Labour
1982-83	Baroness Young	Conservative
1992-97	Virginia Bottomley	Conservative
1992-97	Gillian Shepherd	Conservative
1997-98	Ann Taylor	Labour
1997-98, 2007-10	Harriet Harman	Labour
1997-2001	Mo Mowlam	Labour
1997-2003	Clare Short	Labour
1997-2007	Margaret Beckett	Labour
1998-2001	Baroness Jay	Labour
2001-03	Helen Liddell	Labour
2001-02	Estelle Morris	Labour
2001-07	Patricia Hewitt	Labour
2001-07, 2009-10	Tessa Jowell	Labour
2001-07	Hilary Armstrong	Labour
2003-07	Baroness Amos	Labour
2004-08	Ruth Kelly	Labour
2006-09	Hazel Blears	Labour
2006-09	Jacqui Smith	Labour
2007-08	Baroness Ashton	Labour
2008-10	Yvette Cooper	Labour
2008-10	Baroness Royall	Labour
2010-	Theresa May	Conservative
2010-	Cheryl Gillan	Conservative
2010-	Caroline Spelman	Conservative
2010-	Baroness Warsi	Conservative

Source: Centre for Women and Democracy

THE HOME OFFICE

Sex and power: 5,400 women missing from top jobs

A new report, published today by the Equality and Human Rights Commission, shows a continuing trend of women being passed over for top jobs in Britain. More than 5,400 women are missing from Britain's 26,000 most powerful posts.[1]

The report, *Sex & Power 2011*, measures the number of women in positions of power and influence across 27 occupational categories in the public and private sectors.

The Commission's report calculates that at the current rate of change it will take around 70 years to reach an equal number of men and women directors of FTSE 100 companies. It also found it could be up to 70 years before there are an equal number of women MPs in Parliament – another 14 general elections.

Worryingly, the results of this year's report differ very little from those in the previous report of 2008.

Figures from this year's report reveal that, while women are graduating from university in increasing numbers and achieve better degree results than men, and despite level pegging with men in their twenties, they are not entering management ranks at the same rate, and many remain trapped in the layer below senior management.

In media and culture, women represent 9.5 per cent of national newspaper editors (down from 13.6 per cent in 2008)

Among this year's findings were:

In politics women represent:

⇨ 22.2 per cent of MPs (up from 19.3 per cent in 2008);

⇨ 17.4 per cent of Cabinet members (down from 26.1 per cent in 2008);

⇨ 21.9 per cent of members of the House of Lords (up from 19.7 per cent in 2008);

⇨ 13.2 per cent of local authority council leaders (down from 14.3 per cent in 2008).

In business women represent:

⇨ 12.5 per cent of directors of FTSE 100 companies (up from 11 per cent in 2008);

⇨ 7.8 per cent of directors in FTSE 250 companies (up from 7.2 per cent in 2008).

In media and culture, women represent:

⇨ 9.5 per cent of national newspaper editors (down from 13.6 per cent in 2008);

⇨ 6.7 per cent of chief executives of media companies in the FTSE 350 and the director general of the BBC (down from 10.5 per cent in 2008);

⇨ 26.1 per cent of directors of major museums and art galleries (up from 17.4 per cent in 2008).

In the public and voluntary sector, women represent:

⇨ 12.9 per cent of senior members of the judiciary (up from 9.6 per cent in 2008);

⇨ 22.8 per cent of local authority chief executives (up from 19.5 per cent in 2008);

⇨ 35.5 per cent of headteachers of secondary schools (down from 36.3 per cent in 2008);

⇨ 14.3 per cent of university vice chancellors (down from 14.4 per cent in 2008).

Studies have shown that outdated working patterns where long hours are the norm, inflexible organisations and the unequal division of domestic responsibilities are major barriers to women's participation in positions of authority.

The British economy is paying the price for this exclusion. It has been suggested that greater diversity on corporate boards would improve business performance and increase levels of corporate social responsibility.

Commissioner Kay Carberry said:

'The gender balance at the top has not changed much in three years, despite there being more women graduating from university and occupying middle management roles. We had hoped to see an increase in the number of women in positions of power: however, this isn't happening.

'Many women disappear from the paid workforce after they have children, so employers lose their skills. Others become stuck in positions below senior management, leaving many feeling frustrated and unfulfilled. Consequently, the higher ranks of power in many organisations are still dominated by men.

EQUALITY AND HUMAN RIGHTS COMMISSION

'If Britain is to stage a strong recovery from its current economic situation, then we have to make sure we're not wasting women's skills and talents.'

Note

1   This figure is calculated by adding up all the posts held by men and women, halving that figure so that all posts would be shared equally between the two sexes, minus the number of posts held by women.

For a copy of the report go to www.equalityhumanrights.com/sexandpower

17 August 2011

⇨ Information from the Equality and Human Rights Commission: www.equalityhumanrights.com

Gender quotas in Britain

45% Brits disagree with idea of introducing gender quotas in LSE boardrooms.

By Katie Anderson and Hannah Thompson

Almost half of Brits (45%) disagree with the idea of introducing female quotas on the boards of London Stock Exchange companies, our poll has found.

⇨ 45% do not support quotas to get more women onto the boards of large financial companies.

⇨ 30% agree with gender quotas, while a further 25% aren't sure either way.

⇨ 57% of men think that having minimum quotas of women on London Stock Exchange companies isn't a good idea (21% support quotas).

⇨ Compared to a third (33%) of women who oppose the measures (and 38% who support the idea).

The issue of gender quotas has been a subject for renewed discussion in the past few weeks, as a Government inquiry into male boardroom dominance

Well gentlemen, to the matter of female presence on the board ... All those in favour of simply including the tea lady's name?

has recommended that FTSE 100 companies aim for a 25% female boardroom presence by 2015. The report stopped short of advising in favour of compulsory quotas, however.

Best woman for the job?

Lord Davies, who led the review, spoke for change 'to ensure that more talented and gifted women can get into the top jobs in companies across the UK', but he insisted that far from being a simple 'numbers game', there was evidence that companies who had female board members were more profitable. Norway is an example of a country in which gender quotas have been seen by some as a 'tentative success' in getting more women into previously male-dominated leadership positions. 'Boards cannot afford to use only half of the population's brain power,' argued then Minister for business Ansgar Gabrielsen when the quotas were introduced in 2003.

However, the chairwoman of enforcement service firm Rossendales, Julie Green-Jones, has been among those criticising the proposal for gender quotas, saying that appointments 'should be [of] the best person for the job regardless of their gender'. There is also concern that getting companies to put more women on the board will create resentment and lead to a situation where the female director's colleagues, and perhaps the woman herself, will question her actual ability and suitability for the role. 'I personally would feel very uncomfortable if I was in the boardroom [just] because I was a woman,' Green-Jones added.

11 March 2011

⇨ The above information is reprinted with kind permission from YouGov. Visit www.yougov.com for more information.

© *YouGov*

EQUALITY AND HUMAN RIGHTS COMMISSION / YOUGOV

Women on boards

Information from the Department for Business, Innovation and Skills.

Executive summary

In 2010, women made up only 12.5% of the members of the corporate boards of FTSE 100 companies. This was up from 9.4% in 2004. But the rate of increase is too slow.

The business case for increasing the number of women on corporate boards is clear. Women are successful at university and in their early careers, but attrition rates increase as they progress through an organisation. When women are so under-represented on corporate boards, companies are missing out, as they are unable to draw from the widest possible range of talent. Evidence suggests that companies with a strong female representation at board and top management level perform better than those without[1] and that gender-diverse boards have a positive impact on performance. It is clear that boards make better decisions where a range of voices, drawing on different life experiences, can be heard. That mix of voices must include women.

In 2010, women made up only 12.5% of the members of the corporate boards of FTSE 100 companies. This was up from 9.4% in 2004. But the rate of increase is too slow

The importance of improving the gender balance of corporate boards is increasingly recognised across the world. Some countries, including France and Italy, are considering significant action and some, including Norway, Spain and Australia, have made significant steps already.

A report by the Equality and Human Rights Commission (2008) suggested that at the current rate of change it will take more than 70 years to achieve gender-balanced boardrooms in the UK's largest 100 companies. This pace of change is not good enough. Through our extensive consultations we have found that there are a number of reasons for women's low representation on boards, many well-researched and familiar.

Part of the challenge is around supply – the corporate pipeline. Fewer women than men are coming through to the top level of organisations. Part of the challenge is around demand. There are women in the UK more than capable of serving on boards who are not currently getting those roles.

If these challenges are to be met, then chairmen and chief executives of UK companies need to take action, supported by others in the corporate world, including investors and executive search firms. Government must also play a supporting role.

Summary of recommendations

1   All chairmen of FTSE 350 companies should set out the percentage of women they aim to have on their boards in 2013 and 2015. FTSE 100 boards should aim for a minimum of 25% female representation by 2015 and we expect that many will achieve a higher figure. Chairmen should announce their aspirational goals within the next six months (by September 2011). Also we expect all chief executives to review the percentage of women they aim to have on their executive committees in 2013 and 2015.

2   Quoted companies should be required to disclose each year the proportion of women on the board, women in senior executive positions and female employees in the whole organisation.

3   The Financial Reporting Council should amend the UK Corporate Governance Code to require listed companies to establish a policy concerning boardroom diversity, including measurable objectives for implementing the policy, and disclose annually a summary of the policy and the progress made in achieving the objectives.

4   Companies should report on the matters in recommendations 1, 2 and 3 in their 2012 Corporate Governance Statement whether or not the underlying regulatory changes are in place. In addition, chairmen will be encouraged to sign a charter supporting the recommendations.

5   In line with the UK Corporate Governance Code provision B2.4 'A separate section of the annual report should describe the work of the nomination committee, including the process it has used in relation to board appointments.' Chairmen should disclose meaningful information about the company's appointment process and how it addresses diversity in the company's annual report, including a description of the search and nominations process.

6   Investors play a critical role in engaging with company boards. Therefore investors should pay close attention to recommendations 1-5 when considering company reporting and appointments to the board.

DEPARTMENT FOR BUSINESS, INNOVATION AND SKILLS

7 We encourage companies periodically to advertise non-executive board positions to encourage greater diversity in applications.

8 Executive search firms should draw up a Voluntary Code of Conduct addressing gender diversity and best practice which covers the relevant search criteria and processes relating to FTSE 350 board-level appointments.

9 In order to achieve these recommendations, recognition and development of two different populations of women who are well-qualified to be appointed to UK boards needs to be considered:

⇨ Executives from within the corporate sector, for whom there are many different training and mentoring opportunities; and

⇨ Women from outside the corporate mainstream, including entrepreneurs, academics, civil servants and senior women with professional service backgrounds, for whom there are many fewer opportunities to take up corporate board positions.

A combination of entrepreneurs, existing providers and individuals need to come together to consolidate and improve the provision of training and development for potential board members.

10 This steering board will meet every six months to consider progress against these measures and will report annually with an assessment of whether sufficient progress is being made.

Note

1 *Women Matter*, McKinsey & Company, 2007

February 2011

⇨ The above information is reprinted with kind permission from the Department for Business, Innovation and Skills. Visit www.bis.gov.uk for more information on this and other related topics.

© Crown copyright

Who is affected by gender discrimination?

A survey reveals that men feel discriminated against on gender lines, as much as women do.

The annual *Attitudes to Work* study conducted by IFF Research shows that 17% of UK workers feel that men and women are not treated the same at work.

The study surveyed 460 employees and came up with some interesting results. Here are some of the opinions held by UK employees:

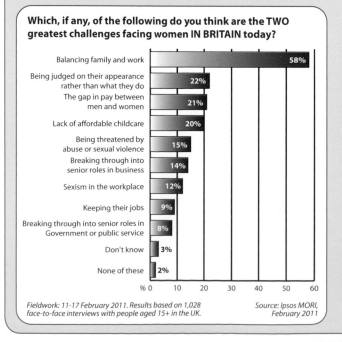

Which, if any, of the following do you think are the TWO greatest challenges facing women IN BRITAIN today?

Balancing family and work	58%
Being judged on their appearance rather than what they do	22%
The gap in pay between men and women	21%
Lack of affordable childcare	20%
Being threatened by abuse or sexual violence	15%
Breaking through into senior roles in business	14%
Sexism in the workplace	12%
Keeping their jobs	9%
Breaking through into senior roles in Government or public service	8%
Don't know	3%
None of these	2%

% 0   10   20   30   40   50   60

Fieldwork: 11-17 February 2011. Results based on 1,028 face-to-face interviews with people aged 15+ in the UK.

Source: Ipsos MORI, February 2011

⇨ 12% believe men are treated better than women.

⇨ 5% believe women are treated better than men.

⇨ 15% of women believe that men are treated better than women.

⇨ 10% of men believe that they are treated better than women.

⇨ 9% of men believe that women are treated better than men.

Joint MD at IFF Research Jan Shury said: 'We are seeing a stark gender divide among those who think discrimination exists. What's even more interesting is the form in which people think discrimination takes place as this also differs greatly between the sexes. Men are seen as having an advantage in remuneration and career progression, whereas women are seen to be ahead in terms of how they are treated at a more personal level.'

11 July 2011

⇨ The above information is reprinted with kind permission from Simply HR Jobs. Visit www. simplyhrjobs.co.uk for more information.

© Simply HR Jobs

Women and decision-making

Representation of women and men in business and government: public attitudes and perceptions – *executive summary*.

By Helen Coombs, Emily Gray and Daniel Edmiston

To help mark International Women's Day on 8 March 2010, the Government Equalities Office commissioned Ipsos MORI to conduct a survey on women's representation in business and government. This report summarises the key research findings from interviews conducted by telephone between 20 and 24 February 2010. Ipsos MORI interviewed a representative quota sample of 1,071 adults in Great Britain aged 16+.

Importance of women and men having an 'equal say' in decision-making

Around three-quarters of the public are in favour of men and women having equal say over decisions. However, people attach different levels of importance to these, dependent on the extent to which people feel the decision affects them directly, and whether there is explicit reference to impact on 'men and women' rather than 'the public as a whole'. It would appear that when people consider decisions about something that will particularly affect them (i.e. local services) or explicitly have a bearing on women and men rather than 'everyone' (i.e. in the workplace), then they place greater importance upon the equal representation of women and men.

People are more likely to say that it is important that women and men have equal say over decisions in the workplace (81%) than with business decisions or political decisions (72% and 73%, respectively). There is least difference between men and women's views with regard to the importance of equal say in decisions that affect local services. There is greatest difference in opinion between men and women with regard to international political decisions.

Women are significantly more likely than men to think that having an equal say is important in decisions about politics, economics, the workplace and local services, while men are significantly more likely than women to say that having an equal say between the sexes is not important.

People are most in favour of a good balance of women and men in making decisions about schools (66%), local councils (64%), the NHS (63%) and in the courts (63%). They are least likely to express a preference for good balance in policing decisions (54%) and economic decisions (55%).

A small proportion of respondents think that women are more suited to decisions about the NHS and health services (6%) and how schools are run (4%). Conversely, over one in ten people think that decisions about how the police fight crime should be mostly made by men (13%) and slightly fewer say the same about finance decisions that affect the economy (7%). There are no significant differences between men and women in these preferences.

Equal representation of men and women in the workplace

When exploring public perceptions about the extent to which it is preferable that different jobs are dominated by one sex, for judges, teachers and doctors, people are more likely to prefer a good balance of men and women working in these roles. Around two-thirds think that there should be a good balance between the sexes in each of these (60%, 66% and 63%). These professions are largely public sector roles and it may be that equal representation is of greater importance to the general public due to this.

By contrast, the public are more divided about engineers and investment bankers. A similar proportion say that it does not matter whether these jobs are mostly held by men or mostly by women and say that there should be a good balance between them, with around two in five people saying it does not matter and the same proportion saying there should be a good balance. A significant minority of people think that investment bankers should be mostly men (9%), while a quarter of the public feel that engineers should be mostly men (25%).

Women are significantly more likely than men to think that there should be a good balance of men and women in jobs. By contrast, men are significantly more likely than women to think that it does not matter which gender holds the majority of positions in different jobs and industries.

Representation of women and men in senior management teams in business

The majority of people in Britain believe that it matters whether men and women are equally represented on the senior management teams that run companies. Agreement that it is preferable for a good balance of men and women to be involved in decision-making on senior management teams tends to be strongest where

IPSOS MORI

they impact upon customers or workplace practices. For example, seven in ten people think that diversity in senior management teams leads to more family-friendly employment practices (71%); this rises to almost three-quarters of women (74%).

Most people agree that 'businesses with a good balance of men and women at senior management level will be better at understanding their customers'. Eight in ten (80%) of people agree, while half strongly agree (50%). This suggests that equal representation of men and women is seen as important in achieving fair outcomes.

Men place less importance upon equal representation on company boards than women. For example, they are significantly more likely to disagree that businesses without women in senior roles are losing out on the best talent (30% compared with 23% of women). Similarly, men are also more likely than women to say that it 'doesn't matter' whether men and women are equally represented (53% compared with 43% of women).

There is a difference in the strength of views of men and women about the importance of equal representation in senior management. While the pattern of agreement between men and women is broadly similar across most of the statements, women tend to be more strongly in favour of equal representation on senior management teams than men. For example, over half of women strongly disagree that because men have more experience in senior management roles, they will be better at running companies (54%), compared with a third of men (33%). However, both men and women attach importance to equal representation in senior management.

Current levels of women in government and business

When presented with evidence of the current level of women in Parliament and on the senior management teams of businesses in the UK, around two-thirds of people think the number of women is too few.

Women are significantly more likely than men to say this is the case in Parliament, although the difference between the views of women and men about current levels of women directors in business is not statistically significant.

The impact of women in government

There is no consensus in the public mind on whether male MPs are as effective as female MPs at representing in Parliament the interests of women in Britain; just over half (54%) of people believe this to be the case. There is no significant difference between the views of men and women.

However, eight in ten people (82%) agree that having women MPs helps to ensure that policies and laws reflect the needs of women, such as on maternity leave and on domestic violence. On this, women are more likely than men to agree (86% compared with 78% of men).

The future of equal representation

When considering the future of equal representation of men and women in different institutions, men and women hold very similar expectations. People do not consider equal gender representation as something that will happen in the short term, i.e. within the next five years. Instead, four out of ten (41%) people think that there will be equal numbers of men and women in Parliament and on senior management teams in five to 20 years time, and 37% of people think it will take this long before there are equal numbers acting as world leaders making international political decisions.

A significant minority (around one in five) think that there will never be equal numbers of men and women in Parliament, senior management teams or acting as world leaders.

March 2010

⇨ The above information is an extract from Ipsos MORI's report *Representation of women in business and government*, and is reprinted with permission. Visit www.ipsos-mori.com for more information.

© *Ipsos MORI*

Be assured that how you do your job will not reflect on our view of women in the profession.

Glass ceiling 'still a barrier to top jobs'

A third of female managers say their gender has hindered career progression.

⇨ Three-quarters of women believe that the glass ceiling still exists.

⇨ Half of women support the introduction of quotas vs a quarter of men.

⇨ Lower confidence and ambition are impeding women leaders' careers.

Almost three-quarters of women (73%) believe the glass ceiling exists and say there are still barriers for women looking to be appointed to senior management and board-level positions in the UK, according to research by the Institute of Leadership & Management released today (21 February 2011). In contrast, just 38% of men believe there is a glass ceiling.

Nearly 3,000 managers were surveyed for the report, *Ambition and Gender at Work*, which reveals that over a third of women (36%) feel that their gender has hindered their career progression. This figure rises to almost half (44%) among those women over the age of 45.

With Lord Davies' review on gender equality in Britain's boardrooms due this week, the research asked whether quotas hold the answer to increasing the number of women in senior roles. While just under half of women (47%) support the idea of quotas, only 24% of men do. Notably, while women over 45 are most in favour of quotas, with almost two-thirds supporting them, men in the same age group are most against.

However, a clear majority of female managers are in favour of a more subtle approach to gender equality in the boardroom and senior management. Almost two-thirds (62%) agreed that 'positive action' should be undertaken to increase the number of women in senior positions, compared with 42% of men.

Responding to the findings of the report, Penny de Valk, Chief Executive of the Institute of Leadership & Management, says: 'The research reveals a real split in opinion on how best to deal with the glacial progress the UK is making towards gender equality. Quotas may be seen as the quickest solution and some countries, notably Norway, have introduced them with some success. However, although they drive compliance, they do not necessarily drive a commitment to the more fundamental changes that are required.

'The imposition of boardroom quotas in the UK would be an admission of failure for leaders. If early predictions about the Lord Davies review are correct, UK plc has two years to increase the number of women on their boards. Rather than waiting for external legislation, now is the time for employers to set voluntary targets for female representation at board and senior management level, and hold people accountable for meeting them. Business leaders must take responsibility for building an effective talent pipeline, and make it a commercial priority to proactively identify, develop and promote potential leaders of both sexes.'

Career aspirations of men and women

The research sheds fresh light on the reasons behind the lack of women in senior management, revealing that women's lower confidence and career ambitions can combine to impede their progress into top roles. Only half of women managers described themselves as having 'high' or 'quite high' levels of confidence, compared to 70% of men. Similarly, just half of women surveyed had expected to become managers when they embarked on their career, compared to almost two-thirds of men. Even among young managers, these gender differences are entrenched, with 45% of men under 30 expecting to become managers or leaders, compared to just 30% of women.

The research also reveals that:

⇨ At every stage the career ambitions of women were found to lag behind those of their male counterparts.

⇨ Fewer women than men have ambitions to reach middle management, department head, general management or director level.

⇨ Women are more likely than men to aspire to run their own businesses, and younger women are the most entrepreneurially ambitious, with a quarter of women under 30 planning to start their own business within ten years.

De Valk continues: 'Our research reveals that women managers tend to lack self-belief and confidence at work compared to their male counterparts. Women feel a greater sense of risk around promotion, which leads to a more cautious approach to career opportunities. And yet we also found that younger women in particular are more likely to aspire to run their own business – they are not adjusting their expectations to the same degree when it comes to the risk of starting their own ventures.

'Employers who are serious about increasing gender diversity at the top need to recognise and respond to these differences, and find ways to nurture women's ambition. This means developing transparent talent management systems and introducing leadership career models and development approaches that flex to meet individuals' differing needs. Coaching and mentoring, in particular, have an invaluable role to play here.

'We know that gender diversity drives organisations' financial performance. Business leaders should need

INSTITUTE OF LEADERSHIP AND MANAGEMENT

no encouragement to realise this competitive advantage by ensuring their most talented employees move into leadership roles, regardless of their gender.'

23 February 2011

⇨ This information is taken from the Institute of Leadership & Management's *Ambition and Gender at Work* research, 2011. Visit www.i-l-m.com/ambitionandgender for more.

Two-thirds of people unhappy with pay gap in their workplace

Two-thirds of people believe the gap between the highest and lowest earners in their workplace is too large, according to polling in a new report published today by IPPR. The report says that government, business and unions should do more to make pay fairer in UK businesses. An overwhelming 78 per cent of people would support government action to reduce the gap between high and low earners, with 82 per cent of those saying government should act in both the public and private sectors.

The report – *Getting what we deserve? Attitudes to pay, reward and desert* – shows that the disproportionate influence of the finance sector is behind much of the massive increase in executive pay over the last 30 years. The report explains how excessive bonuses are paid to a small number of top earners, yet ordinary workers often see no extra money when their organisation is doing well. The new polling shows that half of the public think that bonuses should be awarded on an organisational or team basis, with only a quarter supporting bonuses primarily linked to individual performance.

When asked what the salary of a CEO of a large national company should be, the average answer was £350,579, compared to actual average earnings of £1 million. On average, the public think that CEOs deserve 65 per cent less than they actually earn. Top pay in the public sector is also seen as too high, with people believing that the CEO of a large council should earn 24 per cent less.

The public also say that the low-paid deserve more. Office cleaners – who on average earn £14,000 – should get a 19 per cent pay rise, according to a representative sample of the British population. Similarly, the public say that prison officers – who on average earn £26,800 – should have a 20 per cent pay rise and painters and decorators – on average earning £22,300 – should have a 12 per cent pay rise.

Nick Pearce, IPPR Director, said:

'These polling results show that pay in Britain is out of kilter with the public's sense of just rewards. People think you should get paid what you deserve and don't see the current inequalities as a fair reflection of differences in effort and talent. People want to see the benefits of success more fairly shared within organisations, instead of a few top earners getting an ever bigger share of the pie.

'Executive pay has shot up over the last 30 years but there has been no proportionate rise in the value or performance of companies. Instead, the increasing influence of the finance sector has enabled a small number of top earners to take an increasing share of the wage bill.

'Meanwhile, wages for the bottom half of workers have been stagnating over the last few years. In many organisations, particularly those in the finance sector, pay has become completely disconnected from the effort that people put into their work and the results they achieve. This means that top earners are getting bonuses regardless of performance while ordinary workers see very little reward for their hard work. Government and employers need to find better ways to make sure work is rewarded fairly.'

The report shows how the top ten per cent of earners have seen major rises in their pay over the last three decades. Between 1975 and 2008, the top ten per cent increased their share of the UK's total wage bill from 22 to 32 per cent and the top one per cent of earners more than doubled their share of the wage bill from five per cent in 1975 to 11 per cent in 2008. This disproportionate rise in top pay has been concentrated in Britain's publicly-listed companies: in 2000, FTSE 100 chief executives earned, on average, 47 times the average worker salary, but this had increased to 88 times by 2009. FTSE 100 CEOs earned an average £2.3 million in 2009, and FTSE 250 CEOs had average earnings of £1 million in the same year. The boom in executive pay over the last 30 years came after a 30-year period of very moderate growth among top earners.

The pay gap – measured by the difference between a full-time man earning in the 90th percentile and a man in the 10th percentile – was 2.5 times in 1968 but by 2010, that ratio had risen to 3.7. The pay gap is slightly larger in London – at 4.5 – than the rest of the UK. But the pay gap is particularly wide in London's private sector for both full-time and part-time workers. The 90/10 ratio for full-time private sector workers in London is 4.9 compared to 3.9 among workers across the UK.

9 June 2011

⇨ The above information is reprinted with kind permission from IPPR. Visit www.ippr.org for more information.

INSTITUTE OF LEADERSHIP AND MANAGEMENT / IPPR

Equal pay – the facts

Equal Pay legislation came into force in the UK nearly 40 years ago. But women still earn and own less than men. One in every five women in the United Kingdom lives in poverty. Women are more likely to be employed in low-paid, part-time work. Part-time jobs are typically low paid and have fewer prospects for promotion and access to training.

Even though legislation on implementing equal pay has been in place for 40 years, the gender pay gap in Britain remains among the highest in the European Union. We still have a shocking gender pay gap of 15.5% that hurts women, society and the economy. Removing barriers to women working in occupations traditionally done by men and increasing women's participation in the labour market could be worth between £15 and £23 billion or 1.3 to 2% of GDP.

Did you know...?

⇨ The full-time gender pay gap between women and men is 15.5%.

⇨ The pay gap varies across sectors and regions, rising to up to 55% in the finance sector and up to 33.3% in the City of London.

⇨ Interruptions to employment due to caring work account for 14% of the gender pay gap.

⇨ 64% of the lowest-paid workers are women, contributing not only to women's poverty but to the poverty of their children.

⇨ There are almost four times as many women in part-time work as men. Part-time workers are likely to receive lower hourly rates of pay than full-time workers.

The full-time gender pay gap between women and men is 15.5%

⇨ Nine out of ten lone parents are women. The median gross weekly pay for male single parents is £346, while for female single parents it is £194.

Why do we have pay gaps?

There are converging reasons for why the gender pay gap still exists.

The recession is making things worse

The recession is worsening women's already existing economic inequalities. Even before the recession it was estimated that 30,000 women lose their jobs each year as a result of being pregnant. In the last 12 months, 4.5% of the female workforce experienced redundancy compared with just 3% of men.

Women's worth in the workplace is undervalued

Outdated gender norms and stereotypes around men and women's value in the workplace still exist, which leads to women and men doing different types of work. In addition, men's work is generally given a higher value both socially and economically. Jobs traditionally done by women, such as cleaning, catering and caring, are undervalued and paid less than jobs traditionally done by men, such as construction, transportation and skilled trades.

Discrimination hasn't gone away

40 years since the Dagenham machinists took action and the introduction of the Equal Pay Act, direct and indirect discrimination against women still persists in the workplace. Women council workers in Birmingham recently found out they were missing out on bonuses of

- IT'S BEEN 40 YEARS!!

...DID YOU HEAR SOMETHING?

up to 160% that were being rewarded to those working in male-dominated areas, such as gardening.

The motherhood penalty

Women still do the bulk of caring in the UK. The lack of flexible working and a long working hours culture mean that women pay a penalty at work for their caring role. Added to this, women are often faced with negative attitudes, discrimination and even dismissal in the workplace because of their roles, actual or potential, as mothers and carers.

More women in part-time work

Part-time jobs are typically low paid, with fewer prospects for promotion and access to training. It is the interaction between low pay, part-time work, and the separation of men and women into different types of jobs which hits women hard. However, for women with caring responsibilities, part-time work is not always a matter of choice.

What's Fawcett's solution?

Read our full report *Equal Pay: Where Next?*, produced jointly with UNISON, the TUC and the Equality and Human Rights Commission. Fawcett is calling on the Government to do three things for Equal Pay Day.

In short:

We want the Government to...

Implement the Equality Act 2010 in full, including section 78 which introduces gender pay audits for employers of more than 250 employees from 2013.

Gender pay audits are a key preventative measure to halt the gender pay gap in its tracks, to promote transparency around men and women's pay and to tackle pay inequalities. The Coalition Government is presently considering whether to implement section 78 of the Equality Act. Fawcett is calling for the Government to implement section 78 of the Equality Act 2010 in recognition of the need to tackle the persistent gender pay gap.

We want the Government to...

Extend the right to request flexible working to all employees and work with the Fawcett Society in developing strategies to change employer attitudes and work with business to implement change on equal pay.

Patterns of work and caring are changing for women, who are entering the workplace in larger numbers than ever before, and make up 49% of the workforce. Women still do the bulk of caring work in the UK for children and elderly people. However, 48% of parents feel they do not have a choice about whether to spend their time with their children or at work. Lack of flexible working

opportunities often mean that women pay a penalty at work for their caring role and lose out on promotions, training opportunities and job progression more generally. Therefore, flexible working arrangements should be in place to support the evolving patterns of work and caring for both women and men.

We want the Government to...

Encourage shared parenting through promoting a system of flexible parental leave that considers the potential impact on maternal health and women's potential future earnings.

The Government must encourage shared parenting through promoting a system of flexible parental leave, as committed to in its Coalition Programme published in May 2010. Women's disproportionate caring responsibilities are a key factor in the discrimination faced by women at work. There is little support or encouragement for fathers to spend more time caring. This is bad for fathers, mothers and children who would benefit if care was shared more equally.

⇨ The above information is reprinted with kind permission from the Fawcett Society. Visit www.fawcettsociety.org.uk for more information.

© Fawcett Society

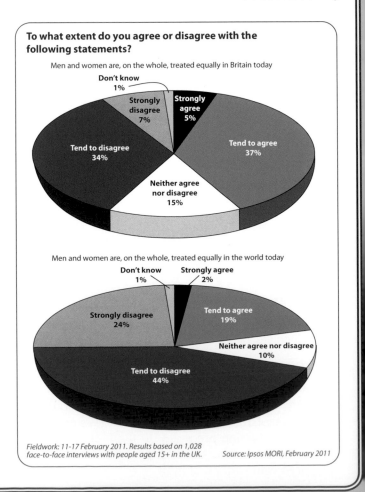

To what extent do you agree or disagree with the following statements?

Men and women are, on the whole, treated equally in Britain today

- Don't know 1%
- Strongly disagree 7%
- Strongly agree 5%
- Tend to agree 37%
- Neither agree nor disagree 15%
- Tend to disagree 34%

Men and women are, on the whole, treated equally in the world today

- Don't know 1%
- Strongly agree 2%
- Tend to agree 19%
- Neither agree nor disagree 10%
- Tend to disagree 44%
- Strongly disagree 24%

Fieldwork: 11-17 February 2011. Results based on 1,028 face-to-face interviews with people aged 15+ in the UK. Source: Ipsos MORI, February 2011

FAWCETT SOCIETY

We can't afford this obsession with the 'gender pay gap'

The alleged pay gap is simply not comparing like for like – men and women make different life choices, says Ruth Porter.

The latest gender pay statistics have provoked the usual storm of nonsense. Apparently, the Government should increase regulatory burdens on businesses, at a time when our economy is seriously faltering. Along with employers, government should also ensure women at work are 'nurtured', whatever that means. Surely it is time we moved on to a proper reasoned discussion about these figures.

Contrary to the Fawcett Society spin, these figures do not show that the patriarchal oppressors are subjugating women at every opportunity they get. In fact they show a diverse picture where people make different choices and there are financial consequences for those decisions. Yes, there are more women in lower-paid jobs. Yes, there are more women in part-time roles and yes, those roles tend to pay less. Yet, according to these latest figures female junior executives are now being paid an extra £602 on average compared to male executives at the same level. What does this actually show? Crucially it reveals that people make different decisions about what they want from a job and how they want to live. It also shows that people have different experiences and skills they bring to a job. It is reasonable to expect that an employer will reward people differently depending on the skills and experience they have.

One publication asserts: 'The average woman will be cheated out of £330,000 in her lifetime. That is 717 Vivienne Westwood tartan Bedrock bags.' Putting aside the outrageous triviality of such a statement (as if women can only understand something if there is a fashion metaphor involved), it is also simply not true. The alleged pay gap is simply not comparing like for like. People are not robots. If these statistics allow us to make any generalised statements about the trends of choices women make, it may be they show us that women do tend to take more responsibility with regard to childcare and elder care, and they do tend to opt to put family above career. These are vast stereotypes though, conflating many different people making many different choices. Even then the data tell us nothing about why different women make different choices.

Much of the commentary around these figures has included the predictable outcry that women must be financially independent just in case a relationship breaks down. Alongside this has been the assertion that women are clearly oppressed and forced into taking the bulk of caring and domestic responsibilities in relationships. There are any number of explanations for these statistics showing more women in low-paid jobs, but if these two reasons are genuine factors as to the figures reading as they do, then we have much bigger problems to worry about than employee pay.

Is our society really at such a point that we can no longer trust that a family relationship will last or that if it does break down people will not agree a fair and sustainable way to move forward? Is it really true that most relationships are in such disarray that a couple cannot negotiate between themselves fair choices that they are both happy with about how to share care for children, elderly relatives and domestic chores?

A headline-grabbing calculation from this new data is that: 'If male and female salaries continued to increase at current rates, it would be 2109 – 98 years – before the average salary for female executives catches up with that of their male peers.' But why should we be worried if it takes another 200 years or indeed if it never happens? People are different, diversity should be celebrated and people should have the freedom to make different decisions.

The Equality Act has certainly increased the burden of red tape on businesses at a time when they can least afford it. But this obsession with the gender pay gap and the consistent misrepresentation of the figures is not something our society can afford. We live in a country where people should feel free to be who they want to be and to do, within certain limits, what they like. Regardless of gender, people should be able to make decisions about what skills to get, what job to do and how to look after their children and elderly parents, free from the constraint of government forcing businesses to pretend these decisions had never been made.

The Government can do some things well, but it should not do anything about these gender pay figures. It is up to people to make the decisions they want to make and yes there will be financial consequences. There may be all kinds of cultural factors feeding in to the decisions women are making but these are best dealt with by honest debate within families, not by some government diktat.

Ruth Porter is the Communications Director at the Institute of Economic Affairs.

1 September 2011

Working mothers and the effects on children

Information from the Economic and Social Research Council.

Parents struggling to combine paid work with bringing up their children now have some positive news thanks to a new study funded by the Economic and Social Research Council (ESRC) on maternal employment and child socio-emotional behaviour in the UK. The research shows that there are no significant detrimental effects on a child's social or emotional development if their mothers work during their early years.

The ideal scenario for children, both boys and girls, was shown to be where both parents lived in the home and both were in paid employment. For children living with two parents, the impact of the working life of the mother may partly depend on the father's own working arrangements. However, using data from the UK Millennium Cohort Study, the researchers discovered that the relationship between behavioural difficulties and employment of the mother was stronger for girls than for boys and that this was not explained by household income, level of mother's education or depression in the mother.

While boys in households where the mother was the breadwinner displayed more difficulties at age five than boys living with two working parents, the same was not true for girls. Girls in traditional households where the father was the breadwinner were more likely to have difficulties at age five than girls living in dual-earner households.

The principal researcher in this study, Dr Anne McMunn, has said: 'Mothers who work are more likely to have higher educational qualifications, live in a higher-income household, and have a lower likelihood of being depressed than mothers who are not in paid work. These factors explain the higher levels of behavioural difficulties for boys of non-working mothers, but the same was not true for girls.'

As previous research has indicated, children in single-mother households and in two-parent households in which neither parent was in work were much more likely to have challenging behaviour at age five than children where both parents were in paid employment. Household income, however, and maternal characteristics, can mitigate the effects of this.

'Some studies have suggested that whether or not mothers work in the first year of a child's life can be particularly important for later outcomes. In this study we did not see any evidence for a longer-term detrimental influence on child behaviour of mothers working during the child's first year of life,' states Dr Anne McMunn.

Notes

1 This press release is based on the findings from 'Maternal employment and child socio-emotional behaviour in the UK: longitudinal evidence from the UK Millennium Cohort Study' funded by the Economic and Social Research Council and carried out by Dr Anne McMunn and researchers from the International Centre for Lifecourse Studies in Society and Health (www.ucl.ac.uk/icls) at UCL.

2 Methodology: The project used data from the UK Millennium Cohort Study (MCS) which is a prospective study of children born in the UK at the start of the new millennium. MCS data are publicly available and ethical approval for data collection was obtained from a multi-centre research ethics committee in the UK.

22 July 2011

⇨ The above information is reprinted with kind permission from the Economic and Social Research Council. Visit www.esrc.ac.uk for more information.

© Economic and Social Research Council

Now that you're five, are you "Developing Difficulties"?

I think "Challenging Behaviours" sounds better!

Car mechanic or cleaner?

Occupational segregation.

Some kinds of jobs, occupations and sectors are dominated by men, and others by women. This is known as occupational segregation and is one of the main reasons why women earn less than men in the UK.

Traditionally, 'women's work' has been considered to be unskilled and inferior and has been undervalued. The result of this is twofold: firstly women are more likely than men to be employed in jobs that are undervalued, and secondly they are more likely to be paid less than men for the same efficiency within the same job.

Women need to be able to work flexibly or part-time so they can balance work and family caring responsibilities. But there are few opportunities for this except in certain occupations which are often low-skilled and low-paid.

Women can easily become trapped in low-skilled and low-paid work and are often working well below their skills levels and their potential. This has a long-term negative impact on their income and contributes to the fact that women experience poverty throughout their lives, and particularly in old age, to a greater degree than men. This can be very bad for children, as women's poverty and children's poverty are closely connected.

Platform 51 thinks that girls' and women's talents are currently being wasted and that occupational segregation contributes significantly to the gender pay gap. This is not only bad for women; it is also a loss to employers who may not be getting the best person for the job if men and women are doing jobs based on their gender rather than their ability. Increasing the numbers of women in sectors where they are under-represented would help to relieve sector-specific skills shortages, which are damaging to the economy. If action were taken to unlock women's talents, it is estimated the UK economy could benefit by up to £23 billion.

Types of occupational segregation

There are two types of occupational segregation: horizontal and vertical.

Horizontal segregation is when men and women tend to work in different occupational sectors. For example, nearly two-thirds of women work in low-paying occupations such as the 'five Cs' – cashiering, catering, caring, clerical and cleaning – as well as in teaching, health professions such as nursing, and as managers in areas like sales and marketing where employees are of a similar skills level. Women are under-represented in traditionally male-dominated sectors, for example

science, engineering and technology (SET), where only 5.3% of working women are employed. Where women tend to be clustered in a narrow range of low-paid work, men are employed in a wider range of jobs, including better-paid roles with greater chances of progression.

Vertical segregation refers to the positions women and men occupy within the same sector or workplace, with women predominately in lower-valued and lower-paid roles rather than at senior or managerial levels. In financial services, for example, men occupy two-thirds of managerial and senior jobs and nearly three-quarters of professional jobs, whereas women are concentrated in the lower-paid jobs. In the medical workforce, despite the increase in women entering the profession over recent years, few have reached senior leadership positions, and only 28% of consultants are women. The under-representation of women in positions of power due to unexplained barriers is referred to as the 'glass ceiling'.

Gender pay gap and low pay

The gender pay gap, that is the difference in pay between men and women, remains considerable. Despite 40 years of equal pay legislation, Britain has one of the largest gender pay gaps in Europe. Occupational segregation is one of the main reasons for the gender pay gap.

In the UK, nearly 60% of men are in the top half of the hourly wage distribution, while nearly 60% of women are in the bottom half. Jobs done by women are more likely to fall below the minimum wage than jobs done by men. Female-dominated workplaces tend to be less well-paid: recent Government statistics suggest that the more men there are in an occupation, the higher the average wages.

BOARD OF DIRECTORS

Part-time work and caring responsibilities

Women are still the main carers of children and dependent adults, and are more likely to need to work part-time or flexibly to balance their caring responsibilities with paid employment. Jobs that are part-time or flexible tend to be lower-paid, which means that women have a higher chance of being lower-paid than men: around two-thirds of jobs paid at the minimum wage are part-time. In the UK, 43% of women who work do so part-time.

Women are more likely than men to have to spend time out of paid work due to care for dependent adult relatives. This has a major effect on their long- and short-term earnings. 21% of the gender pay gap is explained by the difference in years of full-time work experience between women and men. An additional 16% is due to the effect on wages of having worked part-time or having taken time out of the labour market to look after family.

When women move from full-time to part-time work they often move to roles that do not utilise their qualifications, skills and experiences. Many women find it hard to get part-time work which recognises their skills. It is estimated that over five million women work below their potential because of the lack of quality part-time jobs.

Gender stereotypes, education and information, advice and guidance

Gender stereotyping and assumptions about women's and men's roles and abilities are both a cause and consequence of occupational segregation. Gender stereotypes influence the expectations people have of one another, the choices parents make for their children, and the subjects and career choices that girls and boys make for themselves.

Young women and men can feel a strong aversion to working in sectors traditionally considered to be the domain of the opposite sex. Girls can feel concerned that their friends or family may be shocked or dismayed if they were to choose a job such as plumbing, for example.

Education can often reinforce, or fail to challenge, gender stereotypes, and so girls are deterred from developing skills which could lead to higher qualifications and better-paid jobs. In all European countries, gender roles and stereotypes are one of the main concerns about gender inequality in education.

The lack of action by the Government and the education system to break down gender stereotypes is disappointing. Despite the increasing numbers of girls now achieving high grades in both academic and vocational subjects, young women still tend to choose a narrow range of occupations. Once they have chosen a direction, it can be difficult to change to a new occupation.

Many young women choose traditional occupations because they haven't been told about what else is possible. They need accurate and impartial information about career options and what they can expect to be paid for doing certain kinds of work. Girls are often steered towards low-paid work and training in traditionally 'female' roles, such as hairdressing or childcare. As a result, girls are held back before they have even started, not by their own lack of aspiration, but by the lack of aspirations of those around them.

This limits women's opportunities throughout their lives and it limits their lifetime earnings and earnings potential.

Vocational training and careers

Occupational segregation is especially pronounced in vocational and technical jobs, for example in science, engineering and technology skilled trades, where women formed only 1.1% of the workforce in 2008. Vocational training provides a significant opportunity to close this skills gap, and yet it appears to have been reinforcing occupational segregation among young people.

There is strong gender segregation in apprenticeships which is even higher than in the general workforce. The apprenticeships which have the lowest percentage of female apprentices – electrotechnical (1%), engineering (3%) and construction (1%) are the highest paid. Conversely, the lowest-paid apprenticeships have the highest numbers of young women: hairdressing (92%), health and social care (92%) and childcare (97%). These deeply entrenched patterns of occupational gender segregation in part account for the apprentice pay gap, which stood at 21% in 2007, with the average male apprentice earning £39 more a week than the average female apprentice.

The recent introduction of diplomas shows that young people still choose subjects along traditional gender lines. As a result there are marked disparities in the numbers of boys and girls studying in particular areas. Few girls opt for engineering, IT or construction, for example, and in hair and beauty studies and society, health and development, most of the students are girls. There is often little concerted or effective work to challenge the gender-stereotypical choices that young people make.

Employment practices

For those girls and women who do opt to enter non-traditional training there can be even more barriers to face. They often feel intimidated and isolated, and can struggle to complete their training due to a lack of support. Some are even bullied or harassed. There are few female mentors, role models or women in senior roles in certain male-dominated sectors and this can be offputting for women. Consequently they find it hard to challenge occupational segregation.

PLATFORM 51

Similarly, structural barriers such as recruitment practices, non-family-friendly hours of work, and limited availability of part-time work across grades and occupations, can constrain women's choices. Employers may make assumptions about women's capabilities and reliability, particularly if they have caring responsibilities, and this can influence whether they consider employing or promoting them.

What should be done

Greater action must be taken on the part of the Government, education and training providers, and employers to challenge gender stereotypes which influence expectations about the kind of work that women and men can or should do.

Girls and women need to be supported to build their self-esteem to believe they can do any career they choose, and they need help to raise their aspirations and consider all options. Girls need help to gain a range of skills from a young age so they can find work which suits them and makes the most of their talents and abilities.

Information, advice and guidance must challenge gender stereotypes to encourage more women into non-traditional careers. Advice must be high quality and unbiased so that girls are aware of the difference a choice of career could make to their long-term earning prospects. Those in a position to give advice on careers and training should receive equality training.

Girls and women should receive support and mentoring in vocational training. They should be offered taster sessions and work experience placements in higher-paid sectors.

Tackling occupational segregation must be made a priority in the Government's plans to tackle the gender pay gap.

There should be more affordable and available childcare; and there must be more flexible, high-quality and well-paid part-time work opportunities, both across and within all occupational sectors.

Employers should promote more flexible working patterns, and recognise shared parenting, so that working fathers can actively care for their children and mothers can make more informed choices about how they combine paid work with caring commitments.

What Platform 51 does

Platform 51's women-only centres are a safe place where girls and women can learn in ways that suit them. We run alternative, flexible and tailored education programmes for girls who have left or opted out of formal education, perhaps because they have been bullied or because they are struggling with difficult transitions in their lives.

We inform girls and women about non-traditional careers, raise their aspirations and let them know what is possible. We help them to understand what occupational segregation is and how the choices they make in work may affect their lives and earning potential. We have run 'atypical' careers days to give girls a chance to experience traditionally male-dominated occupations such as building, carpentry and plumbing.

We provide specialist support to help those furthest from employment, including young mothers, women from the gypsy and traveller community, and women with learning disabilities.

We help girls build resilience to prevent them opting out of education in the first place; this gives them the confidence to try again when things have not worked before. Our crèches allow mothers to access our services while their children are cared for.

We campaign for girls and women to get chances to work in traditionally male sectors, and we provide evidence and information to the Government, officials and relevant bodies, such as the Low Pay Commission, to highlight the impact that occupational segregation has on women throughout their lives.

Facts

⇨ Unlocking women's talents could benefit the UK economy by up to £23 billion.

⇨ In 2009, the part-time gender pay gap between men working full-time and women working part-time, was almost 40%.

⇨ Women make up 77% of administrative and secretarial posts, 83% of personal services posts and 65% of sales posts, but only 6% of engineers.

⇨ Women hold just 11% of FTSE 100 directorships.

⇨ 80% of girls would or might be interested in a non-traditional job if they were able to try it first.

⇨ 67% of women in one survey were not aware of the differences in pay between jobs traditionally done by women and men, and 57% said they would have considered a wider range of careers options had they known.

⇨ The above information is reprinted with kind permission from Platform 51. Visit www.platform51.org for more information on this and related topics, or to view references for this article.

PLATFORM 51

All-boys schools are not the answer

Boys are lagging behind girls at school. They need teachers who are able to creatively engage every single child in front of them.

By Oli de Botton

Well-to-do parents are increasingly opting to send their children to single-sex prep schools, reversing the trend of recent years. Last week, Michael Gove told us that we needed to promote a *Dangerous Book for Boys* culture so that boys could be boys again. At the beginning of this month, it (re-) emerged that there were far fewer male teachers in primary schools to act as role models.

Underlying this is anxiety about achievement; recent Department for Education figures show that nearly double the number of boys failed to reach expected standards at seven. The gender gap is more than ten points in English at 11. Behaviour is a worry too. Boys are three-and-a-half times more likely to be excluded, and the figure is worse still if you are a working-class or black boy.

Today's answer to the problem seems to be single-sex schools. Yet debates about their value are both age-old and decidedly unresolved. Proponents argue that keeping boys together allows them to expel their 'boyish' energy more freely – ensuring they are in line and on task. Girls are said to benefit too, with more support to build self-confidence.

But there is also evidence in the other direction. A report commissioned by the Headmasters and Headmistresses conference, which represents top private schools, shows that single-sex schools make little difference to outcomes. What's more, arguing that Eton is a good school because it only admits boys is like saying Wayne Rooney is a good footballer because he wears a nice kit – one does not necessarily lead to the other.

In practice, the single-sex question is a distraction from what really matters. It sounds obvious, but boys (and girls) will do better if they are taught better by teachers who understand their individual needs. That means skilled practitioners using the curriculum creatively to engage and excite every single child in front of them – regardless of their gender. And, incidentally, male and female teachers have equal capacity to get this right.

Of course this is hard, and I can say I fell short many times. But just introducing a gender control on the group isn't going to make it any easier. What about the girl who likes active learning or the boy who is shy? I am not sure they would get a fair deal if our teaching is framed by gender behaviours (whatever they may be). In any case, we want kids to be able to excel in response to all learning environments – not just the ones they are comfortable in. So let girls be boisterous, and boys self-reflect. And let them learn together, taught by the best teachers we can find.

28 September 2010

Single-sex schools breed high hopes

With Ofsted reporting that girls at single-sex schools are more likely than their mixed-school contemporaries to avoid 'stereotypically female' careers, are single-sex schools becoming a force to be reckoned with again? Rebecca Marriage investigates.

A recent Ofsted report reveals that girls at single-sex schools are more likely to avoid preparing for 'stereotypically female' careers than their contemporaries in co-educational schools. Despite a downturn in admissions to all-girls' schools, this report, alongside news that almost a third of independent UK girls' schools are turning out 2012 Olympic hopefuls, suggests that it might be time to sit up and take notice of single-sex schools again.

In the recent Ofsted report *Girls' Career Aspirations*, based on visits to 16 primary schools and 25 secondary schools, including 13 single-sex girls' schools, it has emerged that girls in the UK are receiving poor careers education, making it difficult for them to take informed decisions about their future direction.

It seems that the traditional stereotypes are alive and well. Beauty therapy, childcare and hairdressing – careers which often go hand-in-hand with lower pay and fewer opportunities for progression – generally top the list of career aspirations.

However, the report also revealed that girls in single-sex schools, especially those in selective schools, had 'more positive attitudes to non-stereotypical careers'. In these schools, girls did not view any career as being closed to them and felt that women should be encouraged into roles traditionally held by men.

So, what makes girls' schools so different, and how do they help girls to buck the gender stereotype?

Dr Helen Wright, Head of St Mary's Calne and President of the Girls' Schools Association (GSA), has observed, 'Single-sex schools create a strong space where girls and boys can learn to feel comfortable with who they are, free of the pressure to conform to stereotypical notions of how girls and boys should or should not be, look or act.

'Being apart from each other during the school day seems to give both boys and girls greater self-esteem – which is, of course, at the root of successful long-term relationships with others of both genders.'

Girls' schools in decline?

However, despite evidence that girls' schools offer a successful route out of traditional gender stereotypes, it was reported last year that girls' schools were in decline. *The Good Schools Guide* highlighted that the popularity of all-girls' schools was waning as more parents chose to educate their daughters in mixed-gender classrooms.

Girls' schools now represent 13 per cent of the leading state and independent schools selected for the guide, reportedly the lowest proportion since the list began in 1986, when 27 per cent were girls' schools.

The decline might be attributed to a shift in attitudes towards education, a larger choice of top mixed-gender schools, and a growing perception that learning in a mixed environment encourages more rounded and well-adjusted individuals.

However, with the recent news from the GSA that almost a third of independent UK girls' schools have pupils who are hoping to compete in the 2012 Olympics, Dr Wright disagrees with this last point.

'It's a bit of a cliché for independent girls' schools to say they produce all-rounders, but that's because it's generally true. The days when pupils were expected to follow one path narrowly have gone. We find that the more opportunities girls have to participate in a full programme at school, the more likely they are to excel in many different areas and find an area where they particularly shine.'

The single-sex girls' schools visited in the Ofsted report had strong approaches to challenging stereotypical choices, including the use of positive female role models and successful former students returning to the school to share experiences of work.

Breaking down barriers

Ofsted chief inspector Christine Gilbert supported this, and identified that more schools needed to follow this example when breaking down the barriers to achievement.

'Schools need to develop more opportunities for young women to meet professionals working in non-stereotypical roles, and to learn more about what the job entails through diverse work placements.

'Schools should also consider ways in which mentoring could be used more extensively to support young women.'

It seems that pupils at Truro High School for Girls have been presented with just such an inspiring mentor. Barcelona Olympics veteran (1992 heavyweight women's eight) Caroline Pascoe is now headmistress of the school. Here, young sportswomen are given an in-school academic mentor, a scheme which is supported by the Youth Sports Trust.

So what else has made the difference for the young sportswomen? Lesley Watson, Principal at Moira House Girls' School and chair of the GSA sports committee, suggests that it is the excellent support mechanisms provided by the staff in independent girls' schools – support that is apparently lacking for girls in the co-educational schools in the Ofsted study.

Debate set to continue

The debate over single-sex versus co-educational schooling is likely to rage for years to come, and looks set to become a very personal issue for families.

But evidence continues to grow that girls' schools, in particular, offer raised career aspirations and increase confidence in their own abilities, particularly when it comes to bucking the gender stereotypes, as the Ofsted report confirms.

As research carried out by academics at Stamford University, published in 2002, says, 'Girls ... in the single-sex schools received a benefit from the single-sex school environment in terms of heightened career aspirations.'

Lesley Watson agrees. 'When you look at the schools which have girls competing at international level, there may be a disparity in terms of the facilities and resources that they possess, but the common denominator in all is the support and encouragement they give. Girls are given the opportunity to develop in their individual sports, and academic support is given to enable them to achieve at the highest level. That's what makes the difference.'

Summer 2011

⇨ The above information is reprinted with kind permission from *Re:locate* magazine. Visit www.relocatemagazine.com for more information.

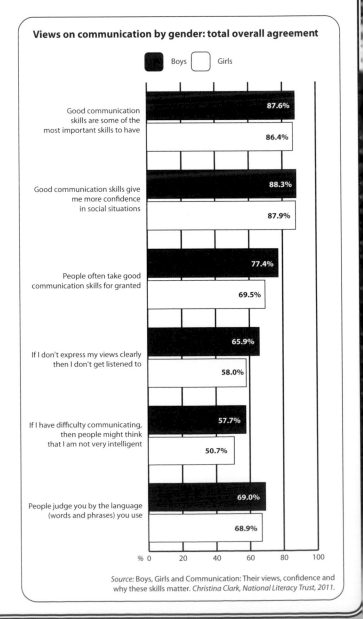

Views on communication by gender: total overall agreement

Boys ▇ Girls ☐

	Boys	Girls
Good communication skills are some of the most important skills to have	87.6%	86.4%
Good communication skills give me more confidence in social situations	88.3%	87.9%
People often take good communication skills for granted	77.4%	69.5%
If I don't express my views clearly then I don't get listened to	65.9%	58.0%
If I have difficulty communicating, then people might think that I am not very intelligent	57.7%	50.7%
People judge you by the language (words and phrases) you use	69.0%	68.9%

% 0   20   40   60   80   100

Source: Boys, Girls and Communication: Their views, confidence and why these skills matter. Christina Clark, National Literacy Trust, 2011.

Women and equality

Information from the NUT.

Introduction

Whilst the last century has seen significant progress in women's empowerment, there are still many inequalities which plague the lives of women today. Black and Minority Ethnic (BME) women in the UK face additional barriers to achieving equality. In common with all women they face gender discrimination, but in addition they are also recipients of racial and religious discrimination.

According to UNICEF:

⇨ 75 million children, of whom 41 million are girls, do not go to primary school.

⇨ Of the world's 796 million illiterate adults, two-thirds are women.

⇨ Data shows that at least one in every three women is a survivor of some form of gender-based violence.

⇨ Girls between 13 and 18 years of age constitute the largest group in the sex industry. It is estimated that around 500,000 girls below 18 are victims of trafficking each year.

⇨ More than 80 per cent of the world's 35 million refugees and displaced people are women and children.

Gender stereotyping

It is important that there is space in the school curriculum to create opportunities to challenge negative gender stereotypes and promote positive role models for young women.

Of the world's 796 million illiterate adults, two-thirds are women

Outdated notions persist about the differences between girls and boys, which lead to expectations of different outcomes, achievements and behaviours based on their sex. These notions limit all young people. Stereotypes put pressure on boys and girls to conform to certain notions of 'masculinity' and 'femininity'. They are a cause of bullying. Often, girls feel they have to decide how far to engage with, or reject, 'girlie' characteristics. Yet generally, girls do not have the skills to enable them to resist the pressures to conform. Boys feel pressurised to commit to dominant forms of masculinity in order to attain popularity and escape censure. These expected forms of masculinity include various combinations of football, fighting, girlfriends, sex, anti-gay talk and misogyny.

Traditional stereotypes still shape young people's aspirations in education, training and employment. The Gender Equality and Race Inclusion project (GERI) have produced teaching resources on challenging occupational gender stereotyping.

Violence against women and girls

The UN declaration on violence against women (1993) defines such violence as:

'Any act of gender-based violence that results in, or is likely to result in, physical, sexual or psychological harm or suffering to women, including threats of such acts, coercion or arbitrary deprivation of liberty, whether occurring in public or private life.'

The vast majority of these violent acts are perpetrated by men on women and girls and include domestic violence, sexual assault, stalking, so-called 'honour-

NATIONAL UNION OF TEACHERS

based violence', female genital mutilation and forced marriage.

Each year across the UK three million women experience violence, and there are many more living with the legacies of abuse experienced in the past.

Figures from the End Violence Again Women YouGov poll (2010) show that almost one in three girls have experienced unwanted sexual touching at school. Nearly three-quarters of the children polled reported hearing sexual name-calling towards girls on an almost daily basis at school.

A key issue concerned with preventing violence against women is the persistence of attitudes that normalise violence against women and girls. Over one in three people believe that a woman should be held wholly or partly responsible for being sexually assaulted or raped if she was drunk.

The inclusion of issues central to gender equality and violence against women and girls in the school curriculum is a vital tool in changing attitudes, and empowering young girls and boys to understand that any form of violence, abuse or controlling behaviour in a relationship must not be tolerated.

The End Violence Against Women Coalition (EVAW) has repeatedly highlighted the sexualisation of women in the media and popular culture as a 'conducive context' for violence against women and has called for action to tackle this. Research shows that adults who viewed sexually objectifying images of women in the mainstream media were more likely to be accepting of violence.

There is a clear link between consumption of sexualised images, a tendency to view women as objects and the acceptance of aggressive attitudes and behaviour as the norm. Using materials and resources that promote positive role models for young men and young women and challenge gender stereotypes can be an important part of examining women's representation in media and popular culture.

Women and poverty

Women are more likely to experience persistent poverty. More than one-fifth of women, 22 per cent, have a persistent low income, compared to approximately 14 per cent of men. Living in persistent poverty denies women the opportunity to build up savings and assets to fall back on in times of hardship. This effect accumulates for older women, which can result in extensive poverty.

For men, economic inactivity is a major route into poverty. This is also true for women, but women face additional poverty risks as a result of their lower earning power, caring responsibilities and changing family structure.

When exploring issues of female poverty you might want to focus on the impact of funding cuts to public services and welfare benefits. Current moves to reduce the deficit have left women facing a 'triple jeopardy' of slashed benefits, job cuts, and a reduction in the core public services that they rely on for themselves and those they care for.

Girls between 13 and 18 years of age constitute the largest group in the sex industry. It is estimated that around 500,000 girls below 18 are victims of trafficking each year

BME women experience considerably higher rates of poverty than white women in the UK. The 2005 Fawcett Society's report on Black and Minority Ethnic Women in the UK highlighted that the incidence of poverty varies greatly between different ethnic groups and is greatest for Pakistani and Bangladeshi women. A number of intersecting factors contributing to women's poverty help explain why BME women are particularly vulnerable:

⇨ lower pay;

⇨ higher rates of unemployment and economic in-activity;

⇨ likelihood of being a single parent;

⇨ likelihood of having a large family.

There is a strong link between female poverty and child poverty. In their report *Gender and Poverty* the Fawcett Society state that women's poverty is closely linked to their family status and caring roles, with women heading their own households, especially lone mothers, at a greater risk of experiencing poverty.

2009 figures produced for the Department for Work and Pensions reveal that 52 per cent of children living in single parent families are poor.

Working mothers are more likely than fathers to be in low-paid jobs. Figures from the Fawcett Society show that 64 per cent of the lowest-paid workers are women, contributing not only to women's poverty but to the poverty of their children.

⇨ There are almost four times as many women in part-time work as men. Part-time workers are likely to receive lower hourly rates of pay than full-time workers.

⇨ Nine out of ten lone parents are women. The median gross weekly pay for male single parents is £346, while for female single parents it is £194.40.

The NUT believes that tackling female poverty should be a key part of any strategy aimed at ending child poverty.

Global issues affecting women and girls

Girls and education

Currently 75 million children, of whom 41 million are girls, do not go to primary school. Education International reports that women and girls face particular obstacles that keep them out of education, including:

⇨ violence on the way to school, in and around schools;

⇨ early pregnancy and early marriage;

⇨ vulnerability to the HIV epidemic;

⇨ discrimination based on gender stereotypes in the wider community and at schools;

⇨ school fees, which may mean that parents send their boys and not their girls to school; and

⇨ lack of gender-sensitive quality education, especially in rural areas.

The United Nations Population Fund (UNFPA) state that education is especially significant for girls and women. This is true not only because education is an entry point to other opportunities, but also because the educational achievements of women can have ripple effects within the family and across generations. Investing in girls' education is one of the most effective ways to reduce poverty. Investments in secondary school education for girls yields especially high dividends. Every one-percentile growth in female secondary schooling results in a 0.3 per cent growth in the economy. Yet girls are often not educated in the poorest countries.

Girls who have been educated are likely to marry later and to have smaller and healthier families. Educated women can recognise the importance of healthcare and know how to seek it for themselves and their children. Education helps girls and women to know their rights and to gain confidence to claim them. However, women's literacy rates are significantly lower than men's in most developing countries.

The 'Send My Sister to School' campaign

The Send My Sister to School campaign, organised by the Global Campaign for Education (GCE), was launched for 2011 to highlight the barriers to education for girls and women. The GCE is inviting UK pupils to become global active citizens and speak out for the education of girls.

Every extra year that a girl gets in school has a great impact on her future. It helps her earn more to escape poverty, keeps her safe from HIV/AIDS, and reduces the risk that her child will die in infancy.

Each year millions of teachers and students from around the world remind their leaders of the important promise they made to get every child into school by 2015.

Equal pay and the Equal Pay Act 1970

The struggle for equal pay lies at the heart of exploring women's campaign for fair and equal rights in the workplace. The TUC-backed 'Union Makes Us Strong' website includes a historical introduction to the campaign for equal pay covering the 1830s, to the introduction of the Equal Pay Act in 1970. The campaign for equal pay has a long history, one which is still ongoing. Women were often a marginalised sector of the workforce and were effectively excluded from many unions until the latter part of the 19th century.

The story of the Women Chainmakers' fight for a living wage provides ideal opportunities for challenging traditional attitudes about women's place in society. In 1910 the Women Chainmakers of Cradley Heath formed a trade union and won the first minimum wage agreement after a strike battle lasting for ten weeks. This increased the wages of the poorest workers by some 150 per cent and remains today one of the most inspiring tales of workers' struggle.

Women's low pay is rooted in long-standing assumptions about a woman's place. The jobs women do attract lower wages. Mary Macarthur's story, and her dedication to improving conditions for working women, form an ideal route into a study of past campaigns for equal pay.

The Equal Pay Act

On 7 June 1968, 850 women machinists working at the Ford Factory in Dagenham went on strike for equal pay after discovering they were being paid 15 per cent less than men for doing the same work. The demands of these women paved the way for the enactment of equal pay legislation in 1970. You might want to look at both equal pay and the position and status of British women in the late 1960s. The Film Education charity has produced digital teaching materials exploring the film *Made in Dagenham*. The TUC has produced a series of films about the fight for equal pay. They include oral history interviews with women and union representatives involved in some of the major equal pay cases since 1968, including the film *A Woman's Worth: the Story of the Ford Sewing Machinists*.

The Equal Pay Act 1970 gives an individual the right to the same contractual pay and benefits as a person of the opposite sex in the same employment, where the man and the woman are doing:

⇨ like work; or

⇨ work rated as equivalent under an analytical job evaluation study; or

⇨ work that is proved to be of equal value.

NATIONAL UNION OF TEACHERS

The Equal Pay Act has now become part of the 2010 Equality Act.

The first effect of the Equal Pay Act 1970 was to remove separate lower women's rates of pay. Before 1970, it was common practice in the private sector and some parts of the public sector for there to be separate, and lower, women's rates of pay. So, for example, at the Ford Motor Company, before a new pay structure was introduced in 1967, there were four grades for production workers:

⇨ male – skilled;

⇨ male – semi-skilled;

⇨ male – unskilled;

⇨ female.

The only significant group of female production workers at Ford were sewing machinists, who were paid less than male toilet cleaners and stores workers.

The Equal Pay Act introduced an 'implied equality clause' into all employees' contracts. This had the effect of eliminating separate lower women's rates of pay. All such rates had to be raised to at least the lowest male rate over a five-year period between 1970 and 1975.

Some employers got round the legislation, for example, by raising the women's rates to the lowest male rate, even when the women's jobs were more demanding than the men's, or by creating different job titles for the women. Despite these strategies, full-time women's average earnings compared to men's rose by five per cent, from 72 per cent to 77 per cent, over a five-year period in the 1970s – the biggest ever increase in this ratio.

Nearly 40 years after the introduction of the Equal Pay Act 1970 the struggle for equal pay still persists. The gender pay gap in Britain remains among the highest in the European Union, with women earning 15.5% less than men. The Fawcett Society estimates that removing barriers to women working in occupations traditionally done by men and increasing women's participation in the labour market could be worth between £15 and £23 billion or 1.3 to 2 per cent of GDP.

The Equal Pay Act has now become part of the Equality Act 2010. The Act brings together nine separate pieces of legislation, including the Sex Discrimination Act, the Race Relations Act and the Disability Discrimination Act, simplifying the law and strengthening it in important ways to help tackle discrimination and inequality.

Unfortunately, a section of the Equality Act that would have given powers to make companies disclose pay differences between men and women, if by 2013 they continued to show no evidence of tackling them, has been removed. This removal of the threat of disclosure may lead to a decline in the closing of the gap between men and women's pay.

The right to vote

There is a wealth of information and resources to draw upon when looking at the history of women's rights in Britain. The 20th century saw an incredible change in the roles of women. At the start of the century women were denied a voice and a vote and were told that their place was in the home.

In 1867 the London Society for Women's Suffrage was formed to campaign for female suffrage. The women's suffrage movement was one of the few political movements in the history of Britain to cut across all classes – for no women could vote regardless of her position. The right for women to vote in 1918, the Representation of the Peoples Act, allowed women over 30 the right to vote. It would take a further ten years to abolish the age qualification. This was a milestone in women's fight for equality and laid the foundations for the 1928 victory which saw women gaining the right to vote on equal grounds to men.

International Womens' Day

International Women's Day is a day to celebrate the role of women in the community and wider society. International Women's Day has its roots in the labour movement at the beginning of the 20th century. The first International Women's Day was launched on 8 March 1911 in Copenhagen by Clara Zetkin, leader of the 'Women's Office' for the Social Democratic Party in Germany. International Women's Day was honoured for the first time in Austria, Denmark, Germany and Switzerland on 19 March. More than one million women and men attended IWD rallies campaigning for women's rights to work, vote, be trained, to hold public office and end discrimination.

Annually on 8 March, thousands of events are held throughout the world to inspire women and celebrate women's achievements. A global web of rich and diverse local activity connects women from all around the world, ranging from political rallies, business conferences, government activities and networking events through to local women's craft markets, theatrical performances, fashion parades and more.

There are a wide range of materials available to help schools celebrate International Women's Day. The United Nations Cyber School bus website contains material and lesson activities on International Women's Day.

⇨ The above information is reprinted with kind permission from the National Union of Teachers. Visit www.teachers.org.uk for more information.

© National Union of Teachers

NATIONAL UNION OF TEACHERS

Ten reasons why it's hard to be a woman

Information from the United Nations Association of the UK.

1. Women perform 66% of the world's work and produce 50% of the food but earn only 10% of the income and own just 1% of the property.

2. Despite progress, men still outnumber women in paid work, and women are often relegated to vulnerable forms of employment, with inadequate earnings, benefits and working conditions. The share of women in paid non-agricultural employment is still languishing at 20% in South Asia, North Africa and Western Asia. In the UK, more than 40 years after the Equal Pay Act, women working full-time are still paid an average of 15.5% less per hour than men – the equivalent of men being paid all year round while women work for free after 2 November.

3. Though the proportion of female representatives in national parliaments worldwide continues to rise slowly, it still stands at just 19%. Women also account for just 16% of ministerial posts. At 20% and 17% respectively, the figures for the UK are not much better than the global averages. Only 18 countries currently have elected female heads of state or leaders.

4. Just a quarter of the world's senior officials or managers are women. Only 13 of the 500 largest corporations in the world have a female CEO and nearly half of all FTSE 250 companies do not have a single woman on their board.

5. Of the 759 million adults across the world who cannot read or write, the vast majority – close to 70% – are women. This proportion has barely changed during the past 20 years. Girls also form the majority of the estimated 72 million children who are not in school.

6. Every 90 seconds, a woman dies in pregnancy or due to childbirth-related complications. That is more than 350,000 deaths each year, 99% of which occur in developing countries: nearly all are preventable.

7. For women and girls aged between 16 and 44, violence is a major cause of death and disability. One woman in three is thought to have been beaten, coerced into sex, or otherwise abused in her lifetime, usually by someone known to her. In some areas of the Democratic Republic of the Congo, 40 women and girls are raped every day. An estimated 200,000 rapes have taken place in the country over the past decade. The perpetrators of the Rwandan genocide committed between 250,000 and 500,000 rapes, while during the conflict in Sierra Leone there were 50,000 such attacks, with a similar number committed over the course of the war in Bosnia. Yet sexual violence remains the least-condemned war crime, in terms of cases brought before court and the low conviction rate.

8. Women's participation in peace negotiations remains patchy – under 8% of negotiators, mediators and witnesses are female. Fewer than 3% of signatories to peace agreements are women and no women have been appointed chief or lead mediators in UN-sponsored peace talks.

9. An estimated 130 million girls and women alive today have undergone female genital mutilation, often in unsafe and unsanitary conditions, and the UN Population Fund believes that each year some 5,000 women are victims of 'honour killings'.

10. While the UN Convention on the Elimination of All Forms of Discrimination against Women has achieved almost universal ratification, states have lodged more 'opt out' clauses against it than to any other human rights treaty.

⇨ The above information is reprinted with kind permission from the United Nations Association of the UK. Visit www.una.org.uk for more information.

© United Nations Association of the UK

Why aren't girls in schools?

Men still dominate women in every country in the world, resulting in widespread discrimination against women and girls. The impact of unequal power relations and discrimination is often felt most severely when material poverty exists, as this increases vulnerability. Inequality in society inevitably has an impact on the provision and content of education, as well as on the ability of girls to enter, and remain in, school.

Gender discrimination

Cultural and social beliefs, attitudes and practices prevent girls from benefiting from educational opportunities to the same extent as boys. There is often a powerful economic and social rationale for investing in the education of sons rather than daughters, as daughters are perceived to be less valuable once educated, and less likely to abide by the will of the father, brother or husband. In most countries, both the public and private sectors continue to be dominated by men, leading parents to ask themselves: why bother educating our girls if they will never make it anyway?

Early marriage and pregnancy

The low value attached to girls' education reinforces early marriage and early pregnancy, keeping girls and their children trapped in a vicious cycle of discrimination. Too often marriage is seen as a higher priority than education, and the girls who are married (even where they have been forced into early marriages against their will), as well as the girls who are pregnant, are excluded from schools.

Violence against girls in schools

Another key issue around rights to and in education concerns the persisting violence against girls. Tragically, this issue is a daily reality for many girls around the world. The violence is not only a direct infringement of human rights as elucidated in the Convention on the Elimination of All forms of Discrimination against Women (CEDAW), but it also plays a role in denying girls the right to access education by being one of the major causes of drop-out among girls. Taken together with the ever-present scourge of corporal punishment and public shaming by school authorities and teachers, a cycle of absenteeism, low self-esteem and violence at home and in schools, this perpetuates those cycles of discrimination which education is supposed to challenge and break.

Schools fail to protect the basic rights and dignity of girls. Violence includes rape, sexual harassment, physical and psychological intimidation, teasing and threats. It may occur on the way to school or within the school itself, and is perpetuated by teachers, parents, persons of perceived authority and fellow students. Schools that also fail to provide adequate physical facilities, such as toilets and running water, cause inconvenience to boys, but spell an end to education for girls before education has even begun.

Statistics about the prevalence of violence against girls are hard to find: it remains under-reported, misunderstood and largely unaddressed, both because of the difficulty of researching the issue, and because of the widespread cultural negligence and betrayal of those who have little or no rights in the first place.

Funding

Funding in girls' education is an important issue. No country has yet succeeded in rescuing girls' education from its continued status as the lowest budget priority and one of the least-favoured areas in public policy.

RIGHT TO EDUCATION PROJECT

'The direct costs of sending all children to school are usually too high for poor parents. While primary school tuition fees have now been abolished in many countries, nearly all developing countries still require payment of various kinds; in many cases, these charges are far higher than direct tuition fees. They include: charges for books, stationery, exam fees, uniforms, contributions to 'building funds, levies imposed by the school management committees, informal tips to teachers and travel costs' (Aikma & Unterhalter 2005, 39).

Household poverty and the need to prioritise reduce educational opportunity for girls because they are the first to suffer. The opportunity costs linked to sending girls to school are significant on poor households. Girls' labour is frequently used to substitute for their mothers', e.g. by caring for siblings. The loss of girls' labour during school hours thus has a detrimental impact on such families' ability to raise their household income, either through food production or wage labour.

Child/domestic labour

Girls are usually 'needed at home' and/or 'need to earn money'. These are major reasons why poor girls drop out of school in most countries. Girls being employed as child labour, bearing the main burden of housework and taking on the role of caring for younger siblings, are impacting girls' performance and attendance in schools, and resulting in physical and mental fatigue, absenteeism and poor performance. 'Opportunity costs refer to labour time lost to the parent when the child goes to school. The opportunity costs are usually much higher for girls than for boys, since girls are expected to do more domestic work than boys' (Aikma & Unterhalter 2005, 39-40). While educating a boy is generally seen as a sound investment, sending a girl to school is frequently seen either as bringing no gain at all, or, worse, as an actual waste of resources.

Lack of government schools

Ministry of Education planners do not always take girls' enrolment targets into consideration when determining how many new schools should be built, or the need to secure girls' education. Such deceptions are allowed to flourish, either due to ignorance or simply to bad intentions, despite the fact that education is the one single investment that is most likely to break the cycle of poverty for the family and for society. The need to travel long distances to school is also one of the main barriers for girls, especially in countries where a cultural premium is placed on female seclusion. This is due to concerns for girls' safety and security, and consequently parents are usually unwilling to let their daughters walk long distances to school (Aikma & Unterhalter 2005, 40).

Lack of encouragement

The limited number of female teachers in both primary and secondary schools is a major constraint on girls' education. The presence of female teachers both makes schools more girl-friendly, and provides role models for girls.

It is also documented that there is an inseparable link between the wellbeing of mothers and the wellbeing of their children. Women who were educated in school frequently have fewer children, and are better able to provide healthcare and adequate nutrition for the children they do have. They are also more likely to send their children to school and keep them in a school system.

Despite most countries having age-old policies aimed at recruiting female teachers, so far none have managed to fill these quotas, 'primarily because governments have consistently failed to guarantee the equal rights of women in teaching, failed to challenge cultural prejudice against female teachers, and often failed to develop effective incentives to encourage female teachers to work', in poor or rural areas.

⇨ The above information is reprinted with kind permission from The Right to Education Project. The project is run by ActionAid International in partnership with the Global Campaign for Education and Amnesty International, and supported by the Open Society Institute. Visit www.right-to-education.org for more.

© Right to Education Project

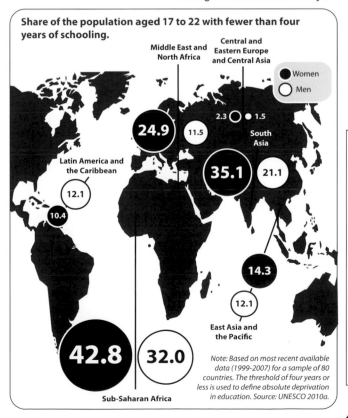

Share of the population aged 17 to 22 with fewer than four years of schooling.

Middle East and North Africa

Central and Eastern Europe and Central Asia

● Women
○ Men

24.9 | 11.5 | 2.3 ○ ● 1.5

South Asia

Latin America and the Caribbean
12.1

35.1 | 21.1

10.4

14.3

12.1

East Asia and the Pacific

42.8 | 32.0

Sub-Saharan Africa

Note: Based on most recent available data (1999-2007) for a sample of 80 countries. The threshold of four years or less is used to define absolute deprivation in education. Source: UNESCO 2010a.

KEY FACTS

⇨ Fewer girls than boys enrol in or complete primary or secondary schooling, even though research shows investing in girls' education significantly improves a country's economic outlook. (page 1)

⇨ Labour laws and regulations in several developing countries actively discourage women from working. When they get a job, women can expect to earn up to 27% less than men for the same job – regardless of experience and education. (page 2)

⇨ A survey identified 60% of fathers now taking, or having taken, paternity leave – with another 23% planning to take it in the future. (page 4)

⇨ An Oxford University study says if current trends continue, women will probably have to wait until 2050 before men are doing an equal share of the household chores and childcare. (page 6)

⇨ A recent survey of 1,000 young girls aged 15 to 19 found 63% considered 'glamour model' to be their ideal profession. A quarter thought lap dancing was a good choice, while only 4% chose teaching. (page 10)

⇨ Women's average pay is 21% less than men's. (page 11)

⇨ Nearly three-quarters of people (73%) say that women who dress in a sexually provocative way are more likely to be harassed. (page 12)

⇨ 51 per cent of the UK's population are women. 22.2 per cent of Members of Parliament are women. (page 13)

⇨ 21 per cent of FTSE 100 companies have exclusively male boards. (page 14)

⇨ A new report shows a continuing trend of women being passed over for top jobs in Britain. More than 5,400 women are missing from Britain's 26,000 most powerful posts. (page 15)

⇨ Almost half of Brits (45%) disagree with the idea of introducing female quotas on the boards of London Stock Exchange companies, a poll has found. (page 16)

⇨ The annual *Attitudes to Work* study conducted by IFF Research shows that 17% of UK workers feel that men and women are not treated the same at work. (page 18)

⇨ Women are significantly more likely than men to think that having an equal say is important in decisions about politics, economics, the workplace and local services, while men are significantly more likely than women to say that having an equal say between the sexes is not important. (page 19)

⇨ The pay gap varies across sectors and regions, rising to up to 55% in the finance sector and up to 33.3% in the City of London. (page 23)

⇨ New research shows that there are no significant detrimental effects on a child's social or emotional development if their mothers work during their early years. (page 26)

⇨ Despite 40 years of equal pay legislation, Britain has one of the largest gender pay gaps in Europe. (page 27)

⇨ Unlocking women's talents could benefit the UK economy by up to £23 billion. (page 29)

⇨ 75 million children, of whom 41 million are girls, do not go to primary school, and of the world's 796 million illiterate adults, two-thirds are women. (page 33)

⇨ Women are more likely to experience persistent poverty. More than one-fifth of women, 22 per cent, have a persistent low income, compared to approximately 14 per cent of men. (page 34)

⇨ Women perform 66% of the world's work and produce 50% of the food but earn only 10% of the income and own just 1% of the property. (page 37)

Equality Act 2010

This act brings a number of existing laws together in one place. It sets out the personal characteristics that are protected by law, and behaviour which is unlawful. The 'protected characteristics' are age; disability; gender reassignment; marriage and civil partnership; pregnancy and maternity; race; religion and belief; sex, and sexual orientation. Under the act people are not allowed to discriminate against, harass or victimise another person because they have any of the protected characteristics.

Gender

Gender is sexual identity, especially in relation to society or culture; the condition of being female or male. Gender refers to socially-constructed roles, learned behaviours and expectations associated with females and males. Gender is more than just biology: it is the understanding we gain from society and those around us of what it means to be a girl/woman or a boy/man.

Gender quotas

A statement that an organisation or body must employ a minimum number of employees from a certain gender, in order to address a lack of male or female representation.

Gender stereotypes

As with other minority groups, people of specific genders are susceptible to stereotyping. Women may be presumed to have a more nurturing nature than men, to care more about their appearance, or to enjoy certain types of books and films ('chick flicks'), among other things. Similarly, people may generalise about men enjoying sports, engaging in 'laddish' behaviour and finding it harder than women to express emotions. In children, this may be manifested as an assumption that the different sexes will prefer different colours and toys.

Glass ceiling

The term 'glass ceiling' refers to the problem of professional advancement sometimes faced by women at work. They are prevented from progressing upwards, in spite of holding relevant qualifications, due to sex discrimination or other factors related to their gender. However, as this barrier is not official it may not be obvious to others.

Occupational segregation

Some kinds of jobs, occupations and sectors are dominated by men, and others by women. This is known as occupational segregation. For example, women may be more likely to work in the caring professions – nursing or childcare, for example – whereas men are more likely to work in manual labour. The undervaluing of what has traditionally been seen as 'women's work' is one of the reasons for the gender pay gap.

Pay gap

The gender pay gap refers to the difference between men and women's earnings. Currently, women earn on average 21% less than their male counterparts.

Sex/gender discrimination

Treating someone differently because they are male, female or transgendered, resulting in a disadvantage to them in a certain area of life, e.g. employment, education.

Sexual bullying

This includes a range of behaviours such as sexualised name-calling and verbal abuse, mocking someone's sexual performance, ridiculing physical appearance, criticising sexual behaviour, spreading rumours about someone's sexuality or about sexual experiences they have had or not had, unwanted touching and physical assault. Sexual bullying is behaviour which is repeated over time and intends to victimise someone by using their gender, sexuality or sexual (in)experience to hurt them.

'SlutWalks'

The 'SlutWalks' were a series of protest marches which began in Toronto, Canada, in April 2011. They then spread to cities around the world. The first march took place after a Toronto police officer suggested that women should 'avoid dressing like sluts' in order to reduce the risk of becoming victims of sexual violence. The marches aimed to make the point that no matter how a woman is dressed, no one has the right to subject her to sexual violence and it is never acceptable to deflect blame away from perpetrators and onto victims. Some of the marchers dressed in revealing clothing to emphasise this point, while others wore their ordinary clothes. The effectiveness of 'Slutwalking' has been hotly debated.

apprenticeships 28
aspirations
   career aspirations 21, 28–9
   girls 10

black and ethnic minority women, and poverty 34
boardroom positions
   gender quotas 16, 21
   women 14, 15, 16, 17–18, 20, 21–2, 37
boys
   and single-sex schools 30
   toy preferences 7–8
bullying, sexual 11

career aspirations 21, 28–9
childcare
   and fathers 4–5
   gender gap 6
child labour, as reason for girls not attending school 39
children
   sexualisation of young girls 9–10
   toy preferences 7–8
   of working mothers 26
colour preferences and gender 7–8

developing countries
   gender inequality 1–2, 35
   girls' education 35, 38–9
diplomas, gender segregation 28
directors, female *see* boardroom positions
discrimination
   definition 3
   at work 18, 23–4
   see also gender pay gap

earnings gender gap *see* gender pay gap
education
   and gender inequality 1
   girls 35, 38–9
   single sex schools 30–32
employment inequality 1–2, 18, 19, 27–9, 37
   see also boardroom positions; gender pay gap
equal pay 23–4, 35–6
   see also gender pay gap
Equal Pay Act 35–6
Equality Act 2010 3, 36
ethnic minority women and poverty 34

fathers 4–5
flexible working 24

gender 1, 11
   and colour preferences 7–8
   and household tasks 6
gender discrimination at work 18
gender equality
   international initiatives 2

legal rights 2, 3
gender inequality 1–2, 33–5, 37
   definition 11
   see also employment inequality; gender pay gap
gender pay gap 22–5, 27–8, 35–6, 37
   reasons for 23–4, 25
gender quotas, company boards 16, 21
gender roles in the home 6
gender stereotyping 11, 33
   employment 23, 28, 29
   toys 7–8
girls
   aspirations 10
   and education 35, 38–9
   sexualisation 9–10
   and single-sex schools 31–2
   toy preferences 7–8
glass ceiling 21–2
government, women in 13, 15, 20, 37

harassment, definition 3
housework, gender gap 6

international initiatives on gender equality 2
International Women's Day 36

legal rights and gender inequality 2, 3, 35, 36
life choices and pay gap 25
literacy rates, women 37

management
   gender gap 19–20
   glass ceiling 21–2
men
   career aspirations 21
   household tasks 6
   paternity leave 4–5
mothers
   and pay gap 24
   working mothers, effect on children 26
MPs, women 13, 15, 20

occupational segregation 19, 27–9

parental leave 4–5, 24
Parliament, women in 13, 15, 20
   worldwide 37
part-time work and gender pay gap 24, 28
paternity leave 4–5
pay gap *see* gender pay gap
politics
   female participation 2, 13, 15, 20, 37
   women's right to vote 36
poverty
   and girls' schooling 39
   and women 34
public appointments, women 14, 15

ACKNOWLEDGEMENTS

The publisher is grateful for permission to reproduce the following material.

While every care has been taken to trace and acknowledge copyright, the publisher tenders its apology for any accidental infringement or where copyright has proved untraceable. The publisher would be pleased to come to a suitable arrangement in any such case with the rightful owner.

Chapter One: Gender in the UK

Gender, © World Bank, *Questions about the Equality Act 2010,* © Equality and Human Rights Commission, *'Family man',* © Fatherhood Institute, *Why women are still left doing most of the housework,* © University of Oxford, *Are pink toys turning girls into passive princesses?,* © Guardian News and Media Limited 2011, *Girls don't want to be princesses. They want to be hot,* © The Vibe, *Stop sexual bullying,* © Womankind 2010, *'SlutWalks' spark debate,* © YouGov.

Chapter Two: Employment and Education

Women's representation, © Crown copyright is reproduced with the permission of Her Majesty's Stationery Office, *Sex and power: 5,400 women missing from top jobs,* © Equality and Human Rights Commission, *Gender quotas in Britain,* © YouGov, *Women on boards,* © Crown copyright is reproduced with the permission of Her Majesty's Stationery Office, *Who is affected by gender discrimination?,* © Simply HR Jobs, *Women and decision-making,* © Ipsos MORI, *Glass ceiling 'still a barrier to top jobs',* © Institute of Leadership and Management, *Two-thirds of people unhappy with pay gap in their workplace,* © IPPR, *Equal pay – the facts,* © Fawcett Society, *We can't afford this obsession with the 'gender pay gap',* © Telegraph Media Group Limited 2011, *Working mothers and the effects on children,* © Economic and Social Research Council, *Car mechanic or cleaner?,* © Platform 51, *All-boys schools are not the answer,* © Guardian News and Media Limited 2010, *Single-sex schools breed high hopes,* © Re:locate.

Chapter Three: The International Situation

Women and equality, © National Union of Teachers, *Ten reasons why it's hard to be a woman,* © United Nations Association of the UK, *Why aren't girls in schools?,* © Right to Education Project.

Illustrations

Pages 8, 23, 31, 37: Simon Kneebone; pages 9, 27: Bev Aisbett; pages 12, 16, 26, 33: Don Hatcher; pages 13, 20, 30, 38: Angelo Madrid.

Cover photography

Left: © Bartek Zielinski. Centre: © B S K. Right: © Evgenia (Jenny) Grinblo.

Additional acknowledgements

With thanks to the Independence team: Mary Chapman, Sandra Dennis and Jan Sunderland.

Lisa Firth
Cambridge
January, 2012

The following tasks aim to help you think through the debate surrounding gender roles and provide a better understanding of the topic.

1 Read the novel 'A Handmaid's Tale' by Margaret Atwood, the story of a future dystopia in which women are virtually enslaved in accordance with an extreme interpretation of Old Testament morality. Write a review, focusing on how the book portrays notions of gender and identity through the character of Offred.

2 'Measures such as gender quotas and all-women shortlists are not ideal, but we do not yet live in a meritocracy and something needs to be done to increase women's participation in corporate and public life.' Do you agree? Write a short essay exploring your views.

3 Watch the film 'Made in Dagenham', which dramatises the events leading to the creation of the Equal Pay Act 1970. Write a review.

4 What is the difference between sex and gender? Create a diagram which could be used in a book for Key Stage 3 pupils, exploring this distinction.

5 'This house believes that the "SlutWalks" drew much-needed attention to the sexual double standard which pervades our society today, and were therefore effective in achieving their aim.' Debate this motion in two groups, with one half arguing in favour and the other against. Carry out some research on the SlutWalk phenomenon before beginning. The article on page 12 provides some background information.

6 Devise a questionnaire to ascertain whether household chores are still split along gender lines among adults of your acquaintance. Find out who would tend to take responsibility for the following within their household: childcare (you may like to divide this into sub-categories); housework such as hoovering, cleaning, washing, ironing and cooking; gardening; car maintenance; DIY; pet care. What conclusions can you draw from your findings?

7 Read *Are pink toys turning girls into passive princesses?* on pages 7-8 and find out more about the Pink Stinks campaign. Visit a children's toy shop, or have a look at their products online. Do you agree that the way toys are colour-coded and marketed reinforces gender stereotypes, or are manufacturers just catering to children's innate tastes? Do you think your own childhood toys influenced the development of your gender identity? Write an opinion piece exploring your views.

8 'Women in the West don't know how lucky they are. They complain of persecution while women in Saudi Arabia, for example, are denied such basic freedoms as the right to drive.' Do you think this is a fair statement? Discuss your views with a partner.

9 Find out about the case of Storm, a Canadian infant who is being raised without an identified gender. What reasons do the child's parents give for their decision? Do you think they are right or wrong to raise their child in this way? Write an opinion piece for your school newspaper or blog, exploring your views.

10 Women are often given cheaper deals on car insurance because they are seen by insurance companies to be statistically safer drivers. Do you think this is fair? Would it be more or less acceptable if similar distinctions were made based on race or sexual orientation?

11 'Feminism is the radical notion that women are people'. Do you agree? Find out about the history of feminism as a political ideology: its origins and its status today.

12 What is the purpose of International Women's Day? How is it observed? Find out about its aims and history.

13 Equalities minister Lynne Featherstone sparked controversy in September 2011 when she implied men were to blame for many of the world's ills, stating 'Look at the mess the world is in, and look who has been in charge'. Is this a fair statement to make? Discuss your views in groups of four (try to have a mix of boys and girls in each group).

14 Design a poster which would encourage young men or women to consider a non-traditional career: for example, childcare for men; engineering for women.